Emerging Market Stocks: Investing in the Global Risk-Return Trade-Off

Amity Sen

Copyright © [2023]
Author: **Amity Sen**
Title: **Emerging Market Stocks: Investing in the Global Risk-Return Trade-Off**

All rights reserved. No part of this book may be reproduced or transmitted in any form or by any means, electronic or mechanical, including photocopying, recording, or by any information storage and retrieval system, without permission in writing from the author.

This book is a product of [**Publisher's Amity Sen**]

ISBN:

Table of Contents

CHAPTER 1. 1
Introduction 1
   1.1. Motivation 1
   1.2. Contribution 2
   1.3. Organization 3
CHAPTER 2. 4
THE IMPACT OF INTERNATIONAL ECONOMIC POLICY UNCERTAINTY, GEOPOLITICAL RISK AND FINANCIAL STRESS ON EMERGING STOCK MARKETS ... 4
   2.1. Overview 4
      2.1.1. Background 4
      2.1.2. Motivation and Literature 5
      2.1.3. Main Contributions 7
   2.2. Estimation Methodology 7
   2.3. Data 9
   2.4. Empirical Results 14
   2.5. Conclusions 16
CHAPTER 3. 27
OIL PRICE SHOCKS AND EMERGING STOCK MARKETS REVISITED 27
   3.1. Background 27
   3.2. Literature review 30
      3.2.1. Oil price shocks and stock returns 30
      3.2.2. Time-varying nature of oil-stock relationship 31
      3.2.3. Oil-stock relationship in oil-exporting and importing economies 32
      3.2.4. Oil-stock relationship in emerging economies 33
   3.3. Data and methodology 34
      3.3.1. Data description 34
      3.3.2. Methodology 37
         3.3.2.1. The VAR model and shock decomposition 37
         3.3.2.2. Markov regime switching model 39
         3.3.2.3. Bootstrapped quantile regression with presence of structural breaks 40

3.4. Empirical Results 42
   3.4.1. Descriptive statistics and time-trends 42
   3.4.2. Linear model results 53
   3.4.3. Markov regime switching model results 59
   3.4.4. Quantile regression model results 64
3.5. Conclusions 70
CHAPTER 4. 72
THE ASYMMETRIC OIL PRICE AND POLICY UNCERTAINTY SHOCK EXPOSURE OF EMERGING MARKET SECTORAL EQUITY RETURNS 72
4.1. Background 72
4.2. Literature Review 75
   4.2.1. Oil prices and emerging economies 76
   4.2.2. Oil prices and sectoral equity returns 77
4.3. Data and Methodology 78
   4.3.1. Data description 78
   4.3.2. Methodology 79
      4.3.2.1. Quantile regression 79
4.4. Empirical Results 81
4.5. Conclusions 94
CHAPTER 5. 96
SUMMARY OF FINDINGS AND SCOPE FOR FUTURE RESEARCH 96

CHAPTER 1
INTRODUCTION

1.1. Motivation

This aims to highlight some relevant aspects of the relationship between the global risk factors and emerging markets (EM) finance. Since, in the last two decades, the emerging stock markets has emerged as preferred investment resorts for investors from developed world. The reasons are higher returns on investment than developed countries and presumably the comparative insulation from catastrophic economic events in developed markets. Thus, to reap the benefits of investment diversification, emerging markets are increasingly preferred over high-income countries. The importance of emerging financial markets as profitable investment avenues were first highlighted by Grubel (1968), followed by Levy and Sarnat (1970) and Errunza (1977). The key argument for including financial assets of EM in the portfolio was to optimize the mean-variance performance, since EM are assumed to yield higher mean returns and lower correlations with developed markets (Bekaert and Harvey, 1997). Besides, the Nobel laureate economist Robert Lucas Jr., in his scholarly work (Lucas, 1990), estimates the expected difference of returns to capital across countries. The results suggest that investments in India is likely to generate 58% more returns than investing in United States. Thus, for investors an emerging economy like India should be a more preferable investment destination.

However, in the recent years, academicians and researchers promulgate a common stochastic behaviour of asset returns across the world. The stronger economic linkages around the world coupled up with developments in information technology systems has eliminated information asymmetries to larger extent (Beine and Candelon, 2011). Thus, the lag time for a market to react in an economy due to spillover of any economic shock in the other part of the world has reduced considerably. Furthermore, developed markets may sniff in the capital flows to emerging markets on occurrence of any undesirable economic event in developed markets. Such an action by investors in developed markets may induce a transmission of economic shock as a domino effect. Thus, due to higher degrees of integration of markets the traditional benefits of investing in emerging markets may erode gradually.

Hence, this intends to draw attention to three intriguing questions related to dynamics of emerging markets finance in form of essays. The first essay is intended to focus upon the question that how the newspaper based Economic Policy Uncertainty (EPU), Geopolitical Risk (GPR) and Financial Stress (FS) of US impact the EM across the various market states. Further, it is also examined whether the shocks of the distinctive nature influence the price and variance risk of the EM stock in a similar way or not. The second essay is focused upon the role of the oil price shocks and its impact on the EM. It must be recognized that the crude oil is a commodity of paramount importance to the EM in order to fuel the process of economic development. Besides, the characteristic feature of fuel-inefficiency due to lack of technological innovations in EM also make these economies vulnerable to the oil shocks. Thus, it is imperative to the oil-stock relationship in the respect of EM. The third essay deals with the asymmetric impact of oil and EPU shocks considering the composite sector level EM equity indexes. It must be realized that considering aggregate country-specific indexes suppress the sectoral characteristics of the stock returns and only the average response is reported to various shocks. Thus, to deepen the understanding further, the sector-specific indexes are considered. In addition, a number of recent studies emphasize that the economic relationships are mostly asymmetric. The stock returns may not respond the same way when the economic shocks are high and when they are low. Therefore, the asymmetric responses are examined and reported in the third essay.

1.2. Contribution

This focuses upon the relationship of global risk factors and EM and contribute the existing literature in a number of ways. Though the plethora of existing studies focus upon the relationship between EPU, GPR and FS, however, the first essay differs from the existing studies and contributes to the literature from a new perspective.[1] Primarily, the compares and contrasts the impact of each stream of shocks upon the EM and explains the results using the theoretical guideline of the information precision theory posited by Pastor and Veronesi (2017) in the context of EPU. Pastor and Veronesi (2017) argue that the investors may consider some nature of information to be relevant and discount the rest. Thus, they might not react to all the information of equal magnitude alike. Thus, the different sources of the macroeconomic shocks such as EPU, GPR and FS may not influence the stock markets in a similar fashion. The results suggest that EPU influences the stock returns relatively more in comparison to GPR and FS. Further, Kelly et al., (2016) assert that the policy related uncertainties could impact the asset prices in two ways i.e. price risk (fall in asset prices) and variance risk (higher volatility in asset prices). The first essay documents that the EPU, GPR and FS have more stronger causalities in price rather than the variance risk. Besides, the heterogeneity of impact across the markets and different conditions is also reported.

The second essay revisits the oil and stock relationship in a new perspective. Though a broad base of existing literature investigates this relationship, however, most of them consider the average oil price changes to examine the empirical relationship. It must be understood that the rise in oil prices could be an outcome of higher demand or due to the higher production costs. Thus, the oil prices could rise because of both demand and supply side shocks. Besides, the relationship of stock returns could be different with such nature of shocks. Nevertheless, most of the previous studies ignore this important consideration or uses the shock decomposition procedure of Kilian (2009). However, Ready (2018) highlights some of the potential shortcomings of the Kilian's (2009) process and suggests a new procedure. It is also important to understand the degree of oil-dependence of each of the countries since the impact of oil price shocks is likely to differ across the oil-importing and exporting countries. Furthermore, the impact of these shocks is likely to be different across the market states. Thus, the second essay uses the novel shock decomposition algorithm of Ready (2018), bifurcates the sample of 24 emerging markets based on the oil-dependence and examines the impact of oil shocks across the different market states. The finds that the demand shocks are positively related to the stock returns, however, the supply shocks are negatively associated with some exception to the oil-exporting countries. The impact of the shocks is found to be profound in the bearish market states.

The third essay focuses upon the asymmetric impact of the oil and EPU shocks on EM composite sectoral equity returns. The sectoral indexes are considered since each of the sector is endowed by its own pedagogical features in terms of market structure, concentration and competition besides its ability/flexibility to pass-over the impact of higher prices to its consumers. Considering the country-specific average indexes shows the average responses,

---

[1] In this introductory chapter the contributions are discussed briefly. The respective chapters discuss the existing literature and contributions in details.

which could be spurious at times. Thus, the sectorial indexes could offer the better estimates of the relationship. It is also worth mentioning that many of the previous and recent literature highlights the fact that the economic relationships are largely asymmetric. Such as Mork (1989) and Mork et al., (1994) documents that rise in oil prices has a definite negative impact on economic output but not otherwise. Hence, the understanding of the asymmetric relationship is important to gain some additional insights. The third essay uses the oil shock decomposition algorithm of Ready (2018) to understand the asymmetric impact of oil and EPU shocks (in addition to some control variables) on the EM composite sectoral equity returns. The finds that the relationship is asymmetric and the magnitude of impact is heterogenous across the sectors.

1.3. Organization

The is comprised of five chapters. The first chapter introduces the central theme of the by highlighting the motivation and contribution of the . The chapters 2, 3 and 4 deals with the three research questions underlined in the motivation section as independent essays. The respective essays outlay the theoretical background, reviews the relevant literature, specifies the methodological approach, discusses the empirical results and concludes. Lastly, chapter 5 is concerned with the summarization of the findings of the three essays and discussion on the scope for the future research.

CHAPTER 2

THE IMPACT OF INTERNATIONAL ECONOMIC POLICY UNCERTAINTY, GEOPOLITICAL RISK AND FINANCIAL STRESS ON EMERGING STOCK MARKETS

This essay addresses the first question and investigates how the several newspaper-based uncertainties such as the Economic Policy Uncertainty, Geopolitical Risk and Financial Stress in US impacts the emerging stock markets. The uses the causality-in-quantiles technique and finds that the causality running from the Economic Policy Uncertainty is profound than the other stream of shocks and mostly causes the price risk.

2.1. Overview

2.1.1. Background

This investigates how the different sources of newspaper-based US macroeconomic shocks influence the asset prices in the emerging stock markets (EMs). The EMs have been the most sought avenues for investment from the developed markets. The relevance of investment in EMs to optimize the mean-variance dynamics of the portfolio was initially highlighted in the late 1960's to 1970's by Grubel (1968), Levy and Sarnat (1970) and Errunza (1977). Since the 1990's, a steady inflow of capital investment to EMs was observed soon after the liberalization of these markets (Bekaert, Harvey, & Lundblad, 2003). Bekaert and Harvey (1997) highlight some differential features of EMs, which may be attributed to the higher inflows of funds such as higher average returns and lower correlations with the developed markets. Prior to the observations of Bekaert and Harvey (1997), using the principles of standard economic theory, Lucas (1990) had also argued that the marginal returns to the capital is higher in relatively poorer economies.

Alternatively, the lenders of the capital from the fund-surplus economies can charge higher rates of interest from borrowers in the fund-deficit economies. Besides, it cannot also be denied that there are certain risks involved with investing in EMs on account of their weaker institutional and regulatory framework as compared to the developed markets (Claessens & Yurtoglu, 2013; Mnasri & Nechi, 2016). Additionally, Bekaert and Harvey (1997) also posit that EMs are also characterized by higher volatilities. Thus, these factors also qualify the investors from the developed world for the additional risk-premium.

The increasing flow of capital across the nations coupled up with decreasing information asymmetries with the evolution of superior information technologies has led the process of capital market integration (Beine & Candelon, 2011). The market integration signifies more synchronized behavior of stock markets across the nations. The higher level of market integration not only diminishes the benefits of international diversification but also induces the risk of adverse economic shock transmissions. Thus, Lehkonen (2015) refers market integration as a double-edged sword. Lehkonen (2015) further argues that the benefits of such globalization of markets were in question, particularly when these well-integrated markets propagated the shocks of the Global Financial Crisis (GFC) across the world. Longin and Solnik (2001) had also claimed that in the phases of high market volatility (or bad market conditions), the international equity markets tend to co-move strongly i.e. a state of market contagion.

Nevertheless, Forbes and Rigobon (2002) suggested that the artefact of contagion is the underlying cross-market linkages that lead to the interdependence. The interdependence between the markets serves as a potential channel to transmit macroeconomic shocks to other markets. In particular, the US being the largest equity market has often been viewed as a barometer of world equity market conditions (Ko & Lee, 2015; Mensi, Hammoudeh, Reboredo, & Nguyen, 2014). Similarly, academic literature in the domain of finance and financial economics have readily recognized the influence of US based shocks on rest of the world (Antonakakis, Chatziantoniou, & Filis, 2013; Colombo, 2013; Das & Kumar, 2018; Ehrmann & Fratzscher, 2009; Ko & Lee, 2015). One of the crucial underlying reasons of this phenomenon is the fact that market participants often attempt to infer information from the other markets (and preferably from the largest markets with lower information asymmetries and the higher degree of corporate governance mechanisms). Thus, the tremors in larger equity markets are not only confined to them.

Unquestionably, foreign investors keep a close vigilance upon the economic and financial conditions of the US. Thus, events such as fluctuations in asset markets or policy related turbulences in the US may be reflected in the behavior of the foreign investors (Su, Fang, & Yin, 2018). The altered behavior of the foreign investors in terms of the future economic outlook and prospects is translated into the changes in asset prices (since there will be a shift in demand and supply equilibrium of asset prices) and increasing volatility. It may be noted that the role of sequential information is primitive in this situation. Thus, in this article, we examine how the US based newspaper indexes of macroeconomic shocks are impacting the EMs. We consider three newspaper-based indexes of distinctive nature, they are Economic Policy Uncertainty (EPU), Geopolitical Risk (GPR) and Financial Stress Indicator (FS). The key question is that these streams of shocks impact the EMs differently or in a similar manner. Addressing to this question will disentangle the nature of shocks that are more detrimental for the EMs. Therefore, the findings may be useful to investors and other market participants to recognize the source of shock, which is more influential on price and variance risk.

2.1.2. Motivation and Literature

The EPU has been a crucial determinant of economic cycle, investment decision and policy making (Bernanke, 1983). Despite of its relevance in the economic system, the earlier empirical researches fail to accommodate this variable since there were no quantitative, continuous and reliable measure of policy uncertainty. To overcome this hindrance Baker, Bloom and Davis (2016) developed a newspaper-based index of political uncertainty. This EPU index has been highly appreciated by the academic community and scholars across the globe used this index to understand the influence of EPU on several perspectives of the economy. For example, firm capital structure (Zhang, Han, Pan, & Huang, 2015), corporate cash holding (Demir & Ersan, 2017), exchange rate expectations (Beckmann & Czudaj, 2017; Kido, 2016), corporate investments (Wang, Chen, & Huang, 2014) and so on.[2]

---

[2] In this we mainly focus upon the relationship of EPU with the stock prices. For a elaborative review of literature on EPU please refer Castelnuovo et al., (2017).

Besides many other aspects of EPU, the relationship with regards to the asset prices has been a prominent field of research. Pastor and Veronesi (2012, 2013) theoretically postulate that the uncertainty in government policies will tend to lower the equity returns. On a similar note, Brogaard and Detzel (2015) empirically argue that the EPU has a negative impact on the equity prices and raises the risk premium. These notable studies were succeeded by an array of empirical literature focusing upon this relationship.[3] Overall the results suggest that EPU causes volatility in stock markets and negatively impacts the stock returns.

This essay is motivated primarily because of two main reasons: (a) the arrival of two new newspaper-based indexes i.e. GPR and FS and (b) the phenomenon of information precision recently put forth by Pastor and Veronesi (2017). The GPR index of Caldara and Iacoviello (2018) primarily focuses on war-like events.[4] Caldara and Iacoviello (2018) compares EPU and GPR indexes and claim that the events captured by this index are more exogenous to business and financial cycles, which could escalate volatilities in the stock markets. Similarly, Püttmann (2018) argues that the events captured by FS index is more focused on the financial aspects of the economy and its scope is not wide as the EPU index. Thus, it becomes interesting to examine that which nature of shock influences the stock prices the most. Thus, the investors and other market participants may understand the nature of events that these markets are more vulnerable to.[5]

Secondly, it may also be noted that these indexes are newspaper-based and voluminous literature using these indexes has also shown that stock prices do react to these indexes. Put differently, the articles related to economic, war or financial uncertainties published in the newspapers has certain impact on stock prices. Thus, the investors react to the arrival of information pertaining to economic uncertainty, risk and stress. Nevertheless, Pastor and Veronesi (2017) observe an anomaly that despite the higher historical EPU levels, the market volatility was low in US, particularly after the US presidential election in November 2016. They associate the phenomenon with the theory of information precision. The economic system is complex and hence there would be many signals (as well as noise) in the market for an investor to perceive and take appropriate actions. With limited humanoid abilities investors may consider only few information signals to be imperative and may discount the rest, which is imprecise. Similarly, some investors may find the news related to the policy uncertainty to be more precise than the war-like events and vice-versa. Thus, the question such as which form of uncertainty information is more precise to the market participants is intriguing and must be answered.

The author uses the non-parametric Causality-in-Quantiles (CQ) approach. The choice of this methodological approach is justified since Kelly et al., (2016) posit that in response to

---

[3] The other relevant studies in this field of literature are as follows: Antonakakis et al., (2013), Raza et al., (2018), Kang et al., (2017), Kang and Ratti (2013), Christou et al., (2017), Arouri et al., (2016), Guo et al., (2018), You et al., (2017), Liu and Zhang (2015), Donadelli (2015), Yang and Jiang (2016), Ko and Lee (2015), Das and Kumar (2018), Tsai (2017), Su et al., (2018) among others.
[4] The brief outline of the GPR and FS indexes are presented in Section 3.
[5] The Federal Reserve Bank of St. Louis and Kansas City had developed their own Financial Stress index, which is based upon the several macroeconomic indicators such as 3-month LIBOR, 3-month treasury bills, swap rates, bank stock prices, S&P 500 returns index and many others. The previous empirical studies largely use these FS indexes (Das, Kumar, Tiwari, Shahbaz, & Hasim, 2018; Gupta, Hammoudeh, Modise, & Nguyen, 2014; Nazlioglu, Soytas, & Gupta, 2015; Reboredo & Uddin, 2016; Sun, Yao, & Wang, 2016). However, as we mention earlier, the FS index of Püttmann (2018) is based on newspaper articles and not on the economic indicators.

political uncertainty events the markets are exposed to two types of risks: (a) drop in stock prices (price risk) and (b) increase in the market volatility (variance risk). The CQ technique captivates the causality of EPU, GPR and FS on the mean and variance of returns. Thus, we are able to capture the causality pertaining to the either type of risks on returns mentioned by Kelly et al., (2016). Additionally, the method also shows the causality at different states of the market i.e. bullish, normal and bearish. The previous literature has established that the economic relationships vary across the different market states (Babalos & Balcilar, 2017; Balcilar, Bonato, Demirer, & Gupta, 2018; Baur, 2013; Das, Bhatia, Pillai, & Tiwari, 2018; Mensi et al., 2014; Mensi, Hammoudeh, & Tiwari, 2016). Thus, understanding the causal relationship at different market states also supplements additional value to the .

2.1.3. Main Contributions

The essay contributes to the literature in three ways. Firstly, it shows that the impact of these shocks is heterogeneous across the markets in terms of causality and intensity. Besides, the impact of the shocks also differs across the different market states. Secondly, the also finds that the influence of EPU is mostly profound and significant as compared to other two shock indicators i.e. GPR and FS. Thirdly, the author reports that the causality-in-mean is more significant and stronger rather than the causality-in-variance. Lastly, the also asserts that the predictability of EPU, GPR and FS is restricted in extreme lower tails. We believe these findings are relevant to the investors in EMs for the purpose of international portfolio diversification and developing investment strategies at the times of turbulent economic conditions.

2.2. Estimation Methodology

The uses the Causality-in-Quantiles (CQ) approach to investigate the causalities running from the EPU, GPR and FS to EMs stock returns.[6] For this purpose, the nonlinear causality approach suggested by Balcilar et al., (2016; 2017) is applied. This method is a typical extension of the models proposed by Nishiyama et al., (2011) and Jeong et al., (2012). This method is advantageous on account of its robustness to capture the general non-linear dynamic dependencies and extreme values (Balcilar et al., 2017). The stock returns of the respective emerging markets is denoted as $y_{(t)}$ and the global exogenous factors i.e. EPU, GPR and FS are denoted as $x_{(t)}$. Thus, the quantile-based causality may be defined following Jeong et al., (2012) as: $x_{(t)}$ does not Granger cause $y_{(t)}$, with respect to the lag-vector of $\{y_{(t-1)}, \ldots, y_{(t-p)}, x_{(t-1)}, \ldots, x_{(t-p)}\}$, in the q-quantile, then we the relationship satisfies the following:[7]

$$Qq(y_{(t)}|y_{(t-1)}, \ldots, y_{(t-p)}, x_{(t-1)}, \ldots, x_{(t-p)}) = Qq(y_{(t)}|y_{(t-1)}, \ldots, y_{(t-p)}) \quad (1)$$

The $x_{(t)}$ is assumed to be the prima facie cause of $y_{(t)}$ in the qth-quantile with respect to $\{y_{(t-1)}, \ldots, y_{(t-p)}, x_{(t-1)}, \ldots, x_{(t-p)}\}$ i

$$Qq(y_{(t)}|y_{(t-1)}, \ldots, y_{(t-p)}, x_{(t-1)}, \ldots, x_{(t-p)}) \neq Qq(y_{(t)}|y_{(t-1)}, \ldots, y_{(t-p)}) \quad (2)$$

where $Qq(y|\bullet)$ implies the qth-quantile of $y_{(t)}$ that depends on t and $q \in (0,1)$.

---

[6] The author is thankful to Dr. Mehmet Balcilar (one of the authors of the CQ R program) for kindly sharing the programming script on our request.
[7] The elaboration of the methodology closely follows Jeong et al., (2012), Balcilar et al., (2018).

Now, let us assume $Y_{(t-1)} \equiv (y_{(t-1)}, \ldots, y_{(t-p)})$, $X_{(t-1)} \equiv (x_{(t-1)}, \ldots, x_{(t-p)})$, $Z_{(t)} = (X_{(t)}, Y_{(t)})$, and $F_{(y_{(t)}|Z_{(t-1)})}(y_{(t)}|Z_{(t-1)})$ and $F_{(y_{(t)}|Y_{(t-1)})}(y_{(t)}|Y_{(t-1)})$ essentially denotes the conditional distribution of $y_{(t)}$ given $Z_{(t-1)}$ and $Y_{(t-1)}$, respectively. For almost all $Z_{(t-1)}$ the conditional distribution $F_{(y_{(t)}|Z_{(t-1)})}(y_{(t)}|Z_{(t-1)})$ is assumed to be continuous in $y_{(t)}$. If we denote, $Qq(Z_{(t-1)}) \equiv Qq(y|Z_{(t-1)})$ and $Qq(Y_{(t-1)}) \equiv Qq(y|Y_{(t-1)})$, in such a case, we have $F_{(y_{(t)}|Z_{(t-1)})}\{Qq(Z_{(t-1)})|Z_{(t-1)})\} = q$ holds with certainty. Hence, the hypotheses for CQ utilizing relations (1) and (2) may be expressed as follows:

$$H_0 : P\{F_{(y_{(t)}|Z_{(t-1)})}\{Qq(Y_{(t-1)})|Z_{(t-1)}\} = q\} = 1 \tag{3}$$

$$H_1 : P\{F_{(y_{(t)}|Z_{(t-1)})}\{Qq(Y_{(t-1)})|Z_{(t-1)}\} = q\} < 1 \tag{4}$$

Following Jeong et al., (2012) the distance measure is employed similarly as follows: $J = \{\epsilon_{(t)} E(\epsilon_{(t)} | Z_{(t-1)}) fz(Z_{(t-1)})\}$, where the error term of regression is given by $\epsilon_{(t)}$ and the marginal density function of $Z_{(t-1)}$ is denoted by $fz(Z_{(t-1)})$. The regression error $\epsilon_{(t)}$ is obtained based on the null hypothesis stated in equation (3), which can be true, under the condition: $\iff$ $E[1\{y_{(t)} \leq Qq(Y_{(t-1)}|Z_{(t-1)})\}] = q$ or equivalently, may be expressed as: $1\{y_{(t)} \leq Qq(Y_{(t-1)})\} = q + \epsilon_{(t)}$, where $1\{\bullet\}$ is an indicator function. Thus, the distance measure may finally be represented as:

$$J = E[\{F_{y_{(t)}|Z_{(t-1)}}\{Qq(Y_{(t-1)})|Z_{(t-1)}\} - q\}^2 fz(Z_{(t-1)})] \tag{5}$$

It is important to note in equation (3) that $J \geq 0$, i.e. the equality will hold if and only if the null hypothesis (H_0) in equation (3) is true, while for the alternative ( ), the condition holds, as specified in equation (4). feasible kernel-based sample analog as shown by Jeong et al., (2012) is given as:

$$\hat{J}_T = \frac{1}{T(T-1)h^{2p}} \sum_{t=p+1}^{T} \sum_{s=p+1, s\neq t}^{T} K\left(\frac{Z_{(t-1)} - Z_{(t-1)}}{h}\right) \hat{\epsilon}_{(t)} \hat{\epsilon}_{(s)} \tag{6}$$

where, the Kernel function with bandwidth h is denoted by $K(\bullet)$. The sample size is T, and the lag order is denoted by p. The unknown estimate of the regression error $\hat{\epsilon}_{(t)}$, is estimated as follows:

$$\hat{\epsilon}_{(t)} = 1\{y_{(t)} \leq \hat{Q}q(Y_{(t-1)})\} - q \tag{7}$$

where the estimate of the qth conditional quantile of $y_{(t)}$ given $Y_{(t-1)}$. Thus, using the nonparametric Kernel method the expression $\hat{Q}q(Y_{(t-1)})$ is estimated as:

$$\hat{Q}q(Y_{(t-1)}) = \hat{F}^{-1}_{(y_{(t)}|Y_{(t-1)})}(q|Y_{(t-1)}) \tag{8}$$

where the Nadarya-Watson Kernel estimator $\hat{F}_{(y_{(t)}|Y_{(t-1)})}(y_{(t)}|Y_{(t-1)})$ is given by:

$$\hat{F}_{(y_{(t)}|Y_{(t-1)})}(y_{(t)}|Y_{(t-1)}) = \frac{\sum_{s=p+1, s\neq t}^{T} L\left(\frac{Y_{(t-1)} - Y_{(s-1)}}{h}\right) 1(y_{(s)} \leq y_{(t)})}{\sum_{s=p+1, s\neq t}^{T} L\left(\frac{Y_{(t-1)} - Y_{(s-1)}}{h}\right)} \tag{9}$$

In (9) the Kernel function is denoted by $L(\bullet)$, and h denotes the bandwidth.

By extending this proposition of Jeong et al., (2012), Balcilar et al., (2016, 2017) developed the test for the second moment. Thus, we can captivate the causality running from economics shocks to the volatility of the stock returns of the emerging markets. The kth moment causality would generally imply the causality in the moment m for $k < m$. The following process of $y_{(t)}$ is considered to illustrate the causality in the moments of higher order.

$$y_{(t)} = g(Y_{(t-1)}) + \sigma(X_{(t-1)})\epsilon_{(t)} \tag{10}$$

The unknown function that satisfies certain stationarity conditions is denoted by $g(\bullet)$ and $\sigma(\bullet)$, whereas $\epsilon_{(t)}$ is a white noise process. Nevertheless, this specification disallows for testing Granger-type causality from $X_{(t-1)}$ to $y_{(t)}$. But when the general nonlinear function is $\sigma(\bullet)$, it could possibly detect the "predictive power" from $X_{(t-1)}$ to $y_{(t)}^2$. Thus, an explicit specification of squares for $X_{(t-1)}$ is not required to define the causality-in-variance. To obtain the causality-in-variance the null and alternative hypothesis is reformulated from equation (10) as:

$$H_0 : P\left[F_{y_{(t)}^2|Z_{(t-1)}}[Q_q(Y_{(t-1)})|Z_{(t-1)}] = q\right] = 1 \tag{11}$$

$$H_1 : P\left[F_{y_{(t)}^2|Z_{(t-1)}}[Q_q(Y_{(t-1)})|Z_{(t-1)}] = q\right] < 1 \tag{12}$$

Thus, in equation (6)-(9) the $y_{(t)}$ is replaced with $y_{(t)}^2$, to achieve a feasible test statistic to test the H_0 in equation (10). Additionally, the approach of Jeong et al., (2012) is adopted to eradicate the problem of causality-in-mean implying the causality-in-variance (Balcilar et al., 2018). Thus, the causality in higher order moments is given by the following equation below:

$$y_{(t)} = g(X_{(t-1)}, Y_{(t-1)}) + \epsilon_{(t)} \tag{13}$$

Hence, the quantile causality of higher order may be specified as:

$$H_0 : P\left[F_{y_{(t)}^k|Z_{(t-1)}}[Q_q(Y_{(t-1)})|Z_{(t-1)}] = q\right] = 1 \text{ for } k = 1, 2, \ldots, K \tag{14}$$

$$H_1 : P\left[F_{y_{(t)}^k|Z_{(t-1)}}[Q_q(Y_{(t-1)})|Z_{(t-1)}] = q\right] < 1 \text{ for } k = 1, 2, \ldots, K \tag{15}$$

The implementation of the quantile causality test necessitates three important specifications: (a) the bandwidth (h), (b) the lag order (p) and (c) the kernel type for $K(\bullet)$ and $L(\bullet)$. In this work, we select a lag order of 1 based on the Schwarz Information Criterion (SIC). In addition, the choice of lag 1 is also congruent with the framework of predictive regressions, which is commonly used for predicting the stock returns (Rapach & Zhou, 2013). The least square cross-validation method is used for selecting the bandwidth value. Lastly, the Gaussian-type kernels is employed for $K(\bullet)$ and $L(\bullet)$

2.3. Data

The considers the major stock indexes of 24 emerging markets as classified by the Morgan Stanley Capital International (MSCI) as on June 2018. The period of the span over 21 years and 5 months of monthly data ranging from January 1997 to May 2018.[8] The

---

[8] The data for some markets does not correspond to the mentioned period (i.e. the data series start from a later starting date) because of its unavailability of data points. The markets are as follows: Colombia (07/2002), Egypt

starting date is constrained by availability of the global EPU data. In addition, the required indexes of EPU, GPR and FS are available in monthly frequency.[9] The dataset for stock prices are extracted from the Bloomberg database. The geographical segmentation specified by MSCI and the respective Bloomberg stock index quotes are presented below in Table 2.1.

Table 2.1. MSCI emerging markets classification

EMERGING MARKETS							
Americas	Index (Bloomberg Quote)	Europe, Middle East and Africa	Index (Bloomberg Quote)	Asia	Index (Bloomberg Quote)		
Brazil	IBOV	Czech Republic	PX	China	SHCOMP		
Chile	IPSA	Egypt	EGX30	India	SENSEX		
Colombia	COLCAP	Greece	ASE	Indonesia	JCI		
Mexico	MEXBOL	Hungary	BUX	Korea	KOSPI		
Peru	SPBLPGPT	Poland	WIG	Malaysia	KLCI		
		Qatar	DSM	Pakistan	KSE100		
		Russia	MICEX	Philippines	PCOMP		
		South Africa	JALSH	Taiwan	TWSE		
		Turkey	XU100	Thailand	SET		
		United Arab Emirates	SASEIDX				

The Table 2.2 exhibits the summary statistics of all the emerging market returns. The returns are calculated as the first logged difference of the respective price indexes. The highest mean return is observed for the Colombian markets. On the other hand, Greek markets show negative mean returns because of the several economic turbulences (such as national budget deficit aftermath 2009, Debt crisis and adoption of austerity measures and so on). The highest standard deviation (SD) of returns is observed for Turkey, whereas the lowest SD is observed jointly for United Arab Emirates (UAE) and Chile. All the markets are negatively skewed (except for the Korean markets), which implies more frequent occurrences of negative values of returns than the positive values. Additionally, the distribution of returns is largely leptokurtic.

Table 2.2. Summary statistics

Countries	Mean	SD	Maximum	Minimum	Skewness	Kurtosis	JB	ADF	PP
Brazil	0.005	0.119	0.374	-0.515	-0.722	5.156	71.561	-14.915	-14.918
Chile	0.005	0.069	0.189	-0.370	-1.106	7.529	269.850	-15.116	-15.147
Colombia	0.013	0.083	0.204	-0.293	-0.482	3.877	13.363	-11.674	-11.738
Mexico	0.007	0.080	0.184	-0.460	-1.267	8.189	354.270	-15.557	-15.577
Peru	0.010	0.088	0.352	-0.502	-0.548	8.382	320.480	-13.580	-13.891
Czech Republic	0.004	0.082	0.224	-0.393	-0.906	6.175	141.950	-13.866	-13.900
Egypt	0.006	0.097	0.356	-0.425	-0.380	5.528	70.295	-13.391	-13.552
Greece	-0.001	0.105	0.335	-0.427	-0.457	4.304	26.817	-14.589	-14.695
Hungary	0.006	0.096	0.232	-0.494	-1.328	7.993	339.840	-14.365	-14.322
Poland	0.005	0.092	0.235	-0.450	-0.881	6.185	140.800	-14.784	-14.784
Qatar	0.008	0.075	0.260	-0.296	-0.404	5.218	54.766	-13.816	13.860

(01/1998), Qatar (08/1998), Russia (05/2001) and Pakistan (03/1998). In addition, the data for FS is available till December 2016.

[9] The dataset for EPU, GPR and FS is accessed from http://policyuncertainty.com.

Russia	0.009	0.101	0.341	-0.313	-0.278	3.858	8.843	-11.607	-11.698
South Africa	0.005	0.077	0.186	-0.403	-1.054	6.415	171.760	-15.428	-15.426
Turkey	0.002	0.138	0.543	-0.547	-0.451	5.582	79.459	-15.959	-15.959
UAE	0.006	0.069	0.179	-0.297	-0.787	5.248	80.009	-12.979	-13.082
China	0.006	0.079	0.278	-0.281	-0.285	4.730	35.264	-14.170	-14.284
India	0.007	0.081	0.311	-0.320	-0.357	4.136	19.139	-14.936	-14.974
Indonesia	0.002	0.121	0.428	-0.667	-1.138	9.365	485.520	-12.892	-12.816
Korea	0.004	0.101	0.393	-0.384	-0.291	5.777	85.541	-14.209	-14.237
Malaysia	0.000	0.080	0.470	-0.332	0.299	10.338	575.930	-13.368	-13.450
Pakistan	0.010	0.087	0.296	-0.415	-0.998	7.393	233.760	-14.542	-14.564
Philippines	0.001	0.082	0.415	-0.338	-0.291	7.202	191.160	-13.080	-13.084
Taiwan	0.001	0.075	0.247	-0.250	-0.186	3.937	10.910	-14.330	-14.376
Thailand	0.002	0.095	0.335	-0.393	-0.584	5.861	101.490	-13.949	-13.978

The Jarque-Bera (JB) test statistic rejects the null hypothesis of normality. It may be easily observed that none of the data series is good-fit for normal distribution. Thus, the quantile-based analysis can provide efficient estimates of causal relationship between the variables at different conditional distributions of the data series. The results for the Augmented Dickey Fuller (ADF) (Dickey & Fuller, 1979) and Phillips Perron (Phillips & Perron, 1988) (PP) test confirms that the data is stationary.

The Figure 2.1 below exhibits the plot of indexes used as the proxy for EPU, GPR and FS. The commonality among these three indexes lays in the fact that they are constructed using similar methodological approach i.e. all the three indexes are newspaper-based. The EPU index is recently developed by Baker et al., (2016), which is also the predecessor of the other two indexes (i.e. GPR and FS).

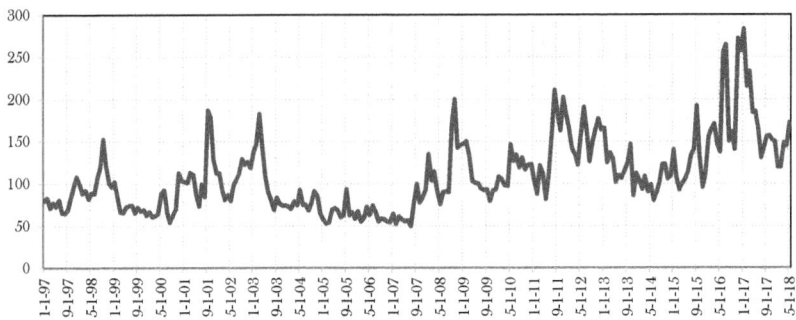

(a) Economic policy uncertainty

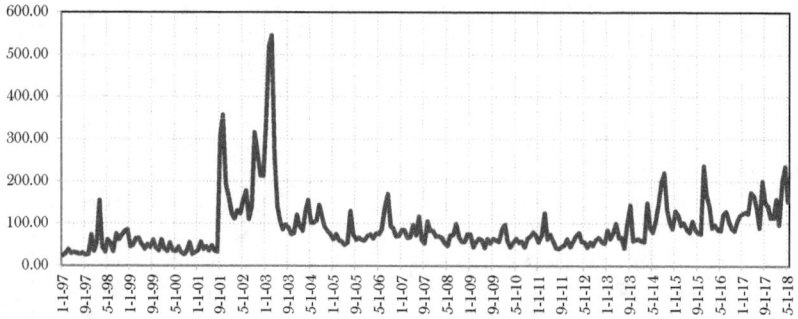

(b) Geopolitical risk

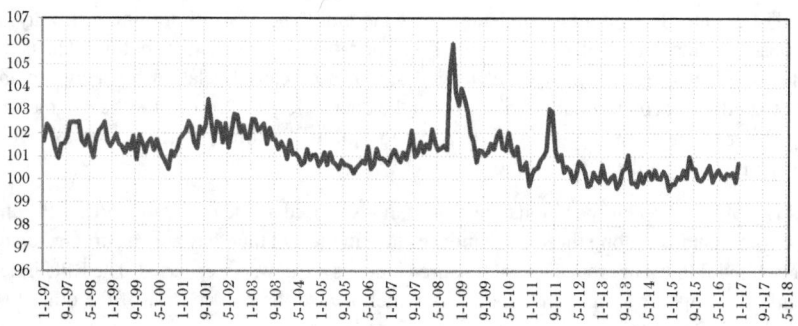

(c) Financial stress

Figure 2. 1. Plot of EPU, GPR and FS index

The EPU index is constructed based upon the newspaper coverage frequency of 10 leading newspapers. The digital archives of each of the newspapers have been searched to derive the monthly count of articles using a specific string of keywords. For example, the articles must contain a trio of terms such as: "uncertain" or "uncertainty"; "economy" or "economic"; in addition to any one of the following terms "deficit", "Congress", "Federal Reserve", "regulation", "legislation", "White House". In short, EPU index corresponds to matters related to economic policies, expected (or actual) changes in government policy and allied matters.

Caldara and Iacoviello (2018) developed the GPR index related to the geopolitical and international political conflicts using a similar approach,. Like the EPU index, the GPR index is also based upon the text-search algorithm considering 11 leading newspapers in the US, UK and Canada. Thus, the articles containing words such as "war", "military", "geopolitics", "terrorism" (and other similar words) are tracked to construct the index.[10] Caldara and Iacoviello (2018) claim that the events, which are exogenous to business and financial cycles

---

[10] Readers are requested to refer Caldara and Iacoviello (2018) for the detailed discussions and methodology of GPR index.

are better captured by the GPR index than the EPU. In addition, the captured events are more likely to sensitize financial volatility and policy uncertainty.

The third index represents the recently developed newspaper-based indicator of the FS by Püttmann (2018). This index is constructed using the five major US based newspapers. To find the frequency of articles featuring in the newspapers a set of predetermined 120 words related to the financial markets were used regarding the "bonds", "business", "central banks", "inflation", "stocks", "trade" etc. Püttmann (2018) argues that the EPU index of Baker et al., (2016) considers all the economic events, which is vague and an abstract idea and also difficult to trace. The FS indicator is precise and plausible concept with ease of categorical tractability (Püttmann, 2018).

Arguably, the nature and sensitivity of these shocks is distinctive. For instance, the highest peak in EPU index (*see* Figure 2.1 (a)) corresponds to the period around December 2016-January 2017, shortly after the US presidential election (November 08, 2016). The maximum historical value of GPR index (*see* Figure 2.1 (b)) corresponds to the year 2003. The underlying attributable reason is the Iraq war (Second Persian Gulf War) that started in 2003. Lastly, the highest value point in FS indicator (*see* Figure 2.1 (c)) corresponds to the GFC of 2008-09. To draw a clear comparison, we compute the mean absolute deviations of the indexes from the historical mean (see Figure 2.2). It can be easily observed that on the event of the US presidential election the deviation of EPU is the maximum as compared to the other two indexes. Similarly, during the Iraq war the deviation is the maximum for GPR index. This clearly indicates the distinctive feature of EPU and GPR index i.e. more responsiveness of EPU and GPR index to political uncertainties and war-like events respectively. However, during the GFC the deviations of EPU and GPR are more than the FS index. As argued by Püttmann (2018) the FS index is refinement of EPU and specifically signifies the financial aspects. Thus, it is possible that the index may not account for the economic and political uncertainties caused by financial strains in the economy.

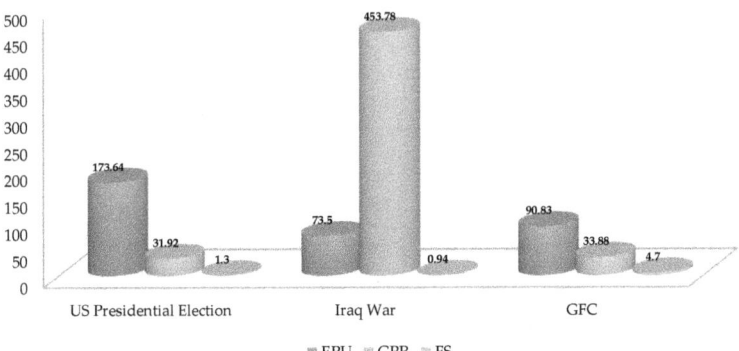

Figure 2. 2. Mean absolute deviations of EPU, GPR and FS on major events

Further, the indexes are also not correlated very strongly. This also indicates that they do not co-move the same way intensely and reactive towards events of different nature. Among the three possible pairs the EPU-GPR exhibits the highest correlation coefficient, whereas the weakest is observed for EPU-FS (*see* Table 2.3).

Table 2. 3. Unconditional correlation between EPU, GPR and FS

	EPU-GPR	EPU-FS	GPR-FS
Correlation coefficient	23.48%	1.86%	9.96%

2.4. Empirical Results

In this section, the author discusses the empirical results on the causal relationship between EPU, GPR and FS and the respective stock market indexes. For the ease and clarity of interpretations we have bifurcated the country indexes based on the geographical segmentation of the MSCI. We designate the quantiles 0.1-0.35 as the bearish, 0.40-0.60 as the normal and 0.65-0.90 as the bullish market states. Table 2.4 and 2.5 reports the causality-in-mean and variance result for the five American EMs i.e. Brazil, Chile, Colombia, Mexico and Peru. For Brazil, the GPR index shows the most significant causalities-in-mean, whereas for the causality-in-variance both EPU and GPR indexes are significant. However, the coefficients are mostly high for the GPR index. The FS index is found to have mostly statistically insignificant results both in mean and variance causality. Further, for Brazil the causality of GPR in mean is mostly significant in the upper tail, which suggests the market is more vulnerable in the bullish state rather than the bearish state. Figure 2.3 exhibits the causality-in-mean and variance from EPU to Brazilian market.[11] The plot clearly indicate that the causality-in-variance is higher than the mean.

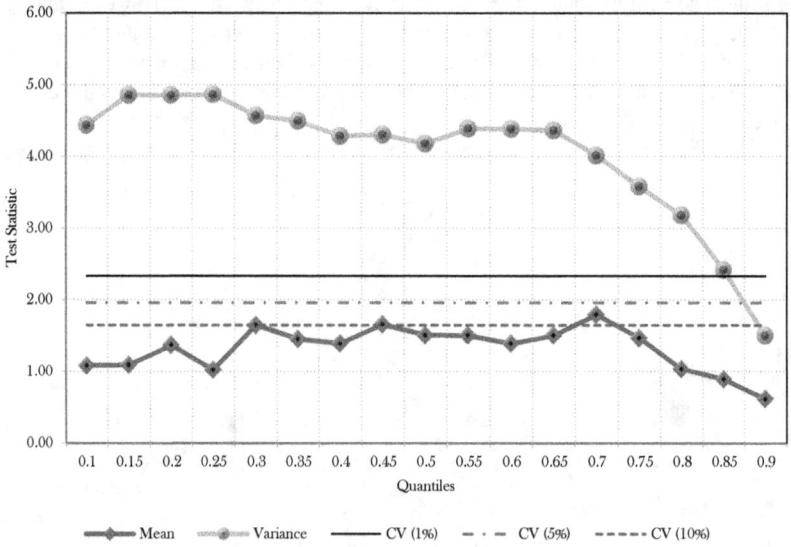

Figure 2.3. The causality-in-mean and variance of EPU to Brazil

---

[11] For parsimony, the author shows the plot only for Brazil.

For Chile, both EPU and GPR are significant for the causality-in-mean. However, the value of coefficients is larger for EPU. The causality-in-variance is statistically insignificant for all three indexes in the case of Chile. In the case of the Colombian markets, the significant causality-in-mean is observed for the GPR index, whereas the causality-in-variance is also insignificant in this case as similar to the Chilean markets. For the markets of Mexico and Peru the causality-in-mean is mostly significant for the EPU. In the case of the causality-in-variance the Mexican markets depict more sensitivity towards the EPU index. On the other hand, Peru's receptivity is more towards the GPR index. Overall, in the American EMs, the mean causality in Brazil and Colombia is significant for GPR, whereas EPU is significant for the other three markets. The higher causality-in-variance due to GPR is observed for Brazil and Peru. The causality-in-variance is statistically insignificant for Chile and Colombia. For Mexico, EPU causes the higher variance for most of the cases.

In the case of the EMs in Europe, Middle East and Africa (*see* Table 2.6 and 2.7) the causality-in-variance is mostly insignificant for Egypt, Greece, Hungary, Poland, Qatar, Russia, South Africa and Turkey. This phenomenon essentially means that in these markets the shocks pertaining to the EPU, GPR and FS impacts more in price drops of rather than causing volatility. In the case of the mean causality Czech Republic, Greece, Hungary, Poland, Qatar and Turkey are more receptive to EPU. Whereas, Egypt, Russia and South Africa, UAE are responsive to FS and GPR index respectively. Colombo (2013), Das and Kumar (2018) have shown previously that the European stock markets and economic activity in Europe is negatively impacted by US based EPU. Our results are consistent with these studies and show significant causalities in mean in European stock markets is influenced by EPU.

In the case of the Asian EMs (*see* Table 2.8 and 2.9), the non-significance of the causality-in-variance is observed for India, Indonesia, Pakistan and Taiwan. The EPU is found to cause in mean in the case of China, Indonesia, Malaysia, Pakistan, Philippines and Taiwan. Whereas, the GPR is found to cause in mean for Korea and Thailand. FS cause in mean only in the case of India. In the case of Indian market Mensi et al., (2014) also report that Indian stock market is insulated of US based EPU. Later on Das and Kumar (2018) also find that the Indian market is more sensitive to the country-specific EPU rather than the US based EPU. The causality-in-variance due to GPR is observed for Korea and Thailand. Malaysia and Philippines are responsive towards the EPU and the variance causality of China originate due to the FS.

Overall, it may be observed that the results are heterogeneous for different countries. Nonetheless, the markets are mostly reactive to EPU index rather than the GPR and FS indexes. The underlying reason could be the fact that as stated by Püttmann (2018), the EPU index is broad and captures many economic fundamentals. On the other hand, the GPR and FS indexes are somewhat narrow and specific to the class of certain events. Moreover, we also find that the stock markets are mostly exposed to the price risk rather than the variance risks, this is consistent with some of the remarkable studies in this domain of literature (Brogaard & Detzel, 2015; Pastor & Veronesi, 2012). The causalities both in mean and variance are mostly significant in the intermediate to higher quantiles, however, the extreme tail dependence is insignificant for most of the cases. In other words, the US macroeconomic shocks fail to cause in mean or variance in the extreme states, which is mostly bearish.

2.5. Conclusions

The compares and contrasts the effect of EPU, GPR and FS on 24 EMs using a nonparametric causality-in-quantiles test. The impetus to undertake this investigation is two dimensional. Firstly, with the increasing recognition of the EPU index in economic literature and the new and more focused indexes are now being constructed, namely, the GPR index by Caldara and Iacoviello (2018) and FS by Püttmann (2018). These indexes are more specialized in the sense that they capture specific events and are expected to have explicit impact on the financial variables. Secondly, Pastor and Veronesi (2017) argue that all the signals available in the market may not be precise to the investors and the market participants. Thus, investors may react to some events and may also discount some events. It may be noted that these indexes (EPU, GPR and FS) are newspaper-based i.e. the information about the future economic outlook is disseminated. Thus, these indexes provide us a reasonable premise to test the information precision hypothesis of Pastor and Veronesi (2017). Hence, it is interesting to investigate that which source of information is assumed to be precise by the investors across different countries.

The finds that the influence of US macroeconomic shocks is heterogeneous across the different EMs, suggesting that the impact these shocks are not uniform across all the markets. However, the influence of EPU is noticed to be more profound both in mean and variance across the continents and countries. Through the lenses of information precision hypothesis of Pastor and Veronesi (2017), we may argue that the overall envelope of economic and policy uncertainty is better perceivable to the investors and market participants rather than the specific war or financial events. In general, the EPU, GPR and FS is found to hold a more consistent impact on mean rather than the variance of returns. This implies that these shocks influence the EMs more in terms of price risk rather than the variance risk. To sum up, the fundamental question we raise in this article is: whether or not the EPU, GPR and FS indexes impact the EMs alike? Our empirical results show that the impact in terms of causality varies across countries, quantiles, magnitude and also in mean and variance.

Table 2.4. Causality-in-mean results for American emerging markets

Quantiles	Brazil			Chile			Colombia			Mexico			Peru		
	EPU	GPR	FS	EPU	GPR	FS	EPU	GPR	FS	EPU	GPR	FS	EPU	GPR	FS
0.1	1.08	1.03	0.70	1.54	2.09**	0.90	1.40	1.09	1.07	0.85	0.95	0.75	1.12	1.26	0.89
0.15	1.09	1.22	1.35	1.74*	2.28**	0.87	1.90	1.33	1.11	1.42	1.04	1.08	1.43	1.34	0.91
0.2	1.37	1.31	1.10	2.30**	2.27**	0.73	1.64	1.47	1.33	1.42	1.49	1.30	1.88*	1.28	0.91
0.25	1.02	1.51	1.34	2.36***	2.98***	0.86	1.52	1.97**	1.25	1.44	1.13	1.48	1.89*	1.21	0.89
0.3	1.65*	1.78*	1.03	2.54**	2.40***	0.95	1.46	1.96**	1.24	1.44	1.46	1.53	2.08**	1.35	1.25
0.35	1.45	1.97**	1.11	2.73**	2.30**	0.90	1.47	1.78*	1.49	1.33	1.38	1.41	1.92*	1.46	1.02
0.4	1.39	2.23**	1.39	3.01***	2.50***	0.87	1.69	1.97**	1.31	1.25	1.56	1.31	2.64***	1.93*	1.19
0.45	1.65*	2.38***	1.31	2.61***	2.20**	1.07	1.71	1.67*	1.25	1.52	1.77*	1.55	3.15***	1.80	1.28
0.5	1.51	2.65***	1.45	2.96***	2.06**	1.30	1.68	1.96**	1.17	1.66*	1.50	1.34	3.37***	1.63	1.60
0.55	1.50	2.23**	1.55	2.91***	2.47***	1.15	1.83	2.11**	1.52	1.89*	1.62	1.43	3.45***	1.49	1.28
0.6	1.39	2.47***	1.48	3.05***	2.10**	1.21	2.02	1.97**	1.34	1.52	1.63	1.45	2.77***	1.51	1.44
0.65	1.50	2.27**	1.42	2.99***	2.04**	0.90	2.07	1.67*	1.24	1.48	1.57	1.39	2.24**	1.53	1.25
0.7	1.79*	2.30**	1.67*	2.59***	1.67*	1.05	1.78	1.17	1.12	1.46	1.51	1.31	1.78*	1.68*	1.33
0.75	1.47	1.96**	1.27	1.97**	1.85*	1.12	1.52	0.96	1.33	1.33	1.25	0.91	1.76*	1.23	1.44
0.8	1.03	1.24	1.29	1.77*	2.17**	0.80	1.34	1.01	1.38	0.96	1.22	0.74	1.64	1.19	1.28
0.85	0.89	1.11	0.86	1.37	1.81*	0.77	1.35	0.78	1.12	0.89	1.32	0.69	1.54	0.83	1.05
0.9	0.61	0.64	0.87	1.24	1.27	0.74	1.01	0.62	0.83	0.65	1.00	0.49	1.00	0.82	0.44

Note: The asterisk indicates the rejection of the null hypothesis of non-causality at the 10% (*), 5% (**) and 1% (***) level of significance.

Table 2.5. Causality-in-variance results for American emerging markets

Quantiles	Brazil			Chile			Colombia			Mexico			Peru		
	EPU	GPR	FS	EPU	GPR	FS	EPU	GPR	FS	EPU	GPR	FS	EPU	GPR	FS
0.1	4.44***	4.17***	0.34	0.35	0.33	0.48	0.42	0.53	0.23	2.72***	2.28**	0.40	0.80	4.11***	0.51
0.15	4.86***	4.93***	0.40	0.31	0.82	0.35	0.54	0.44	0.20	2.72***	2.13**	0.58	0.77	4.85***	0.52
0.2	4.85***	5.09***	0.30	0.25	0.57	0.39	0.57	0.55	0.18	2.95***	2.47***	1.02	0.94	4.76***	0.68
0.25	4.86***	4.84***	0.43	0.25	0.57	0.41	0.68	0.44	0.57	3.53***	2.59***	0.64	0.84	4.69***	0.78
0.3	4.57***	4.94***	0.46	0.30	0.54	0.55	0.83	0.47	0.39	2.99***	2.84***	0.90	0.70	5.09***	0.76
0.35	4.49***	4.94***	0.41	0.45	0.68	0.50	0.82	0.69	0.99	2.94***	3.35***	0.82	0.71	4.83***	0.55
0.4	4.28***	4.82***	0.42	0.53	0.78	0.55	0.80	0.74	0.78	3.29***	3.59***	0.70	1.00	5.00***	0.57
0.45	4.30***	5.13***	0.61	0.35	0.48	0.56	0.71	0.61	0.65	3.21***	3.38***	0.63	0.97	4.91***	0.38
0.5	4.18***	4.93***	0.45	0.35	0.42	0.50	0.87	0.38	0.79	3.47***	3.10***	0.71	0.99	4.73***	0.42
0.55	4.39***	4.97***	0.58	0.33	0.51	0.59	0.88	0.50	0.54	3.36***	2.85***	0.49	0.78	4.61***	0.44
0.6	4.38***	4.42***	0.48	0.55	0.93	0.71	0.77	0.37	0.60	3.20***	2.79***	0.48	0.92	4.47***	0.49
0.65	4.36***	4.16***	0.57	0.48	1.01	0.66	0.67	0.52	0.71	2.83***	2.86***	0.61	0.93	4.36***	0.62
0.7	4.01***	3.92***	0.39	0.34	0.54	0.55	0.52	0.34	0.47	2.71***	2.77***	0.54	0.88	4.08***	0.64
0.75	3.58***	3.68***	0.27	0.48	0.67	0.63	0.45	0.20	0.39	2.27**	2.43***	0.38	0.63	3.81***	0.56
0.8	3.18***	3.29***	0.44	0.41	0.52	0.77	0.44	0.17	0.22	1.89*	2.33***	0.29	0.41	3.44***	0.75
0.85	2.42***	2.30**	0.50	0.19	0.25	0.55	0.46	0.16	0.25	1.64	1.85*	0.27	0.30	2.77***	0.56
0.9	1.50	1.56	0.48	0.24	0.21	0.42	0.35	0.19	0.36	1.35	1.43	0.27	0.32	1.85*	0.43

Note: The asterisk indicates the rejection of the null hypothesis of non-causality at the 10% (*), 5% (**) and 1% (***) level of significance.

Table 2. 6. Causality-in-mean results for Europe, Middle East and African emerging markets

Quantiles	Czech Republic			Egypt			Greece			Hungary			Poland		
	EPU	GPR	FS	EPU	GPR	FS	EPU	GPR	FS	EPU	GPR	FS	EPU	GPR	FS
0.1	1.13	1.26	1.03	1.33	0.88	1.04	1.86*	1.07	1.45	1.08	1.48	0.99	0.76	0.60	0.69
0.15	1.23	1.38	1.15	1.43	1.35	1.21	1.96**	1.21	1.92*	1.05	1.37	0.93	0.90	0.82	0.73
0.2	1.03	1.18	2.03**	1.62	1.18	1.18	1.82*	1.45	1.79*	1.06	1.58	1.13	1.36	1.00	1.23
0.25	1.24	1.20	1.91*	2.08**	1.51	1.55	1.92*	1.88*	1.59	1.23	1.47	1.50	1.01	1.07	1.11
0.3	1.40	1.44	1.92*	2.42***	1.39	2.07**	2.09**	1.88*	1.36	1.43	1.34	1.77*	0.95	1.63	1.22
0.35	1.60	1.52	1.97**	2.24**	1.24	2.89***	2.08**	1.72*	1.60	1.53	1.62	1.39	0.94	1.86*	1.41
0.4	1.36	1.35	1.88*	2.36***	1.35	2.31**	2.23**	1.91*	1.89*	1.55	1.18	1.24	1.11	1.49	0.97
0.45	1.69*	1.61	1.69*	2.05**	1.14	2.31**	2.29**	1.57	1.71*	1.36	1.23	1.18	1.44	1.21	1.04
0.5	1.86*	1.73*	1.89*	1.69*	1.05	2.06**	2.21**	1.85*	1.73*	1.75*	1.40	1.36	2.00**	1.16	1.07
0.55	1.58	1.62	1.79**	1.58	1.40	2.19**	2.65***	1.72*	1.51	2.17**	1.39	1.25	1.54	1.12	0.90
0.6	2.03**	1.43	1.54	1.33	1.70*	1.70*	2.38***	1.43	1.27	1.77*	1.59	1.66	1.60	1.30	1.01
0.65	2.20**	1.50	1.35	1.48	1.73*	1.28	2.31**	1.34	1.33	2.04**	1.09	1.44	0.90	1.23	1.06
0.7	1.92*	1.82*	1.34	1.33	1.46	0.99	1.85*	1.29	1.17	1.79*	1.33	1.46	1.07	1.22	1.35
0.75	2.07**	1.33	1.13	1.31	1.35	0.95	1.59	1.27	1.24	1.38	1.64*	1.36	0.91	1.40	1.25
0.8	1.98**	1.26	1.28	1.63	1.19	0.75	1.15	1.08	1.29	1.21	1.52	1.16	1.02	1.16	1.39
0.85	1.50	0.77	0.95	1.30	0.93	1.03	0.98	1.06	1.13	0.92	1.39	1.30	0.91	1.02	1.50
0.9	1.14	0.85	0.71	0.75	0.62	0.78	0.65	0.70	1.03	0.65	1.14	0.83	1.01	0.65	1.18

Quantiles	Qatar			Russia			South Africa			Turkey			UAE		
	EPU	GPR	FS	EPU	GPR	FS	EPU	GPR	FS	EPU	GPR	FS	EPU	GPR	FS
0.1	1.39	0.93	1.32	0.69	0.91	1.37	0.69	0.94	0.83	1.22	1.02	1.32	1.45	1.57	1.49
0.15	1.68*	1.11	1.13	0.72	1.25	1.38	0.79	1.15	0.88	1.30	0.93	1.06	1.54	1.84*	1.82*
0.2	1.49	1.54	1.54	0.94	1.62	1.54	0.96	1.18	0.81	1.64*	0.90	1.23	1.98*	1.68*	1.55
0.25	1.70*	2.10**	1.56	1.22	1.76*	1.89*	1.09	1.09	0.86	1.19	1.49	1.42	1.76*	1.66*	1.74*
0.3	2.09**	1.93*	1.67*	1.66*	1.83*	1.70*	1.09	1.21	1.02	1.06	1.29	1.72*	1.86*	1.78*	2.11**
0.35	2.24**	1.94*	1.72*	1.36	1.54	1.71*	0.79	1.41	1.03	1.24	1.40	2.06**	1.54	1.88*	2.49***
0.4	1.87*	1.78*	1.39	1.25	1.40	1.93*	0.82	1.55	1.43	1.49	1.40	1.70*	1.62	1.83*	1.75*
0.45	1.92*	1.71*	1.45	1.54	1.60	1.80*	0.98	1.75*	1.20	1.70*	1.99**	1.28	1.90*	1.73*	2.26**
0.5	1.92*	1.69*	1.57	1.74*	1.85*	1.59	1.00	2.31**	1.44	1.73*	2.24**	1.48	1.81*	1.94*	2.14**
0.55	1.94*	1.66*	1.49	1.50	1.73*	1.68*	1.05	2.19**	1.72*	2.07**	1.79*	1.46	1.57	1.92*	2.14**
0.6	2.26**	1.89*	1.30	1.71*	1.75*	1.63	1.47	2.41***	1.39	1.69*	1.72*	1.36	1.79*	2.30**	1.73*
0.65	1.80*	1.90*	1.51	1.53	1.61	1.42	1.24	2.78***	0.95	1.78*	1.38	1.35	1.89*	2.15**	1.62
0.7	1.63	1.49	1.29	1.54	1.31	1.28	1.30	2.23**	0.76	1.57	1.29	1.49	1.70*	2.02**	1.61
0.75	1.79*	1.25	1.23	1.17	0.90	1.35	1.83*	2.03**	0.59	2.09**	1.18	1.24	1.50	1.24	1.57
0.8	1.60	1.18	1.01	1.44	0.74	1.14	1.07	1.43	0.43	1.61	1.39	1.27	1.26	1.00	1.47
0.85	1.64*	1.17	1.18	0.79	0.82	1.26	0.97	1.01	0.75	1.39	0.94	0.67	1.07	0.85	1.33
0.9	1.03	0.91	0.93	0.56	0.63	0.91	0.67	1.30	0.57	0.85	0.79	0.72	0.76	0.77	1.32

Note: The asterisk indicates the rejection of the null hypothesis of non-causality at the 10% (*), 5% (**) and 1% (***) level of significance.

Table 2.7. Causality-in-variance results for Europe, Middle East and African emerging markets

	Czech Republic			Egypt			Greece			Hungary			Poland		
Quantiles	EPU	GPR	FS	EPU	GPR	FS	EPU	GPR	FS	EPU	GPR	FS	EPU	GPR	FS
0.1	2.58***	2.58***	0.74	0.63	0.30	0.31	0.60	0.36	0.32	0.43	0.44	0.44	0.46	0.37	0.42
0.15	2.49***	2.46***	0.91	0.89	0.46	0.34	0.28	0.53	0.42	0.43	0.40	0.59	0.68	0.35	0.35
0.2	2.54***	2.46***	0.84	0.52	0.64	0.37	0.30	0.58	0.50	0.69	0.56	0.57	0.57	0.30	0.30
0.25	3.26***	2.83***	0.77	0.85	0.62	0.43	0.42	0.44	1.01	1.10	0.46	0.66	0.50	0.27	0.30
0.3	3.45***	2.62***	1.10	0.71	0.75	0.47	0.53	0.62	1.80	1.57	0.55	0.56	0.97	0.59	0.36
0.35	3.77***	3.08***	1.22	1.18	1.15	0.39	0.62	0.68	0.82	0.94	0.45	0.52	0.82	0.59	0.34
0.4	3.64***	3.18***	0.90	1.47	0.98	0.78	0.40	0.56	0.87	0.99	0.55	0.67	0.93	0.66	0.45
0.45	3.84***	3.46***	0.98	1.55	0.69	0.57	0.39	0.70	1.10	1.04	0.74	0.53	0.84	0.77	0.51
0.5	4.17***	3.35***	1.30	1.30	0.78	0.48	0.40	1.06	0.89	1.32	0.83	0.57	0.96	0.55	0.59
0.55	4.25***	2.95***	1.07	1.42	1.10	0.37	0.40	0.64	0.98	1.47	1.17	0.58	0.95	0.66	0.57
0.6	4.35***	2.84***	1.44	1.16	0.93	0.37	0.41	0.84	1.56	1.16	0.84	0.45	0.80	0.85	0.65
0.65	4.03***	2.79***	0.92	1.07	1.12	0.45	0.36	0.63	1.41	0.97	0.76	0.72	0.92	0.70	0.60
0.7	3.51***	2.71***	0.82	0.71	0.76	0.46	0.80	1.02	1.60	0.93	0.80	0.56	1.05	0.50	0.88
0.75	3.61***	2.73***	0.68	0.71	0.51	0.23	0.58	0.56	1.03	1.01	0.75	0.62	0.73	0.46	0.81
0.8	3.02***	2.49***	0.61	0.53	0.37	0.22	0.97	0.91	0.77	0.72	0.73	0.45	0.64	0.40	1.05
0.85	2.17**	1.98**	0.48	0.46	0.36	0.37	0.68	0.47	0.89	0.61	0.74	0.48	0.50	0.62	0.61
0.9	1.54	1.67*	0.42	0.30	0.40	0.34	0.63	0.35	0.57	0.50	0.56	0.47	0.36	0.38	0.27

Quantiles	Qatar			Russia			South Africa			Turkey			UAE		
	EPU	GPR	FS	EPU	GPR	FS	EPU	GPR	FS	EPU	GPR	FS	EPU	GPR	FS
0.1	0.66	0.97	0.62	0.14	0.24	0.92	0.93	1.15	0.74	0.16	0.50	0.33	1.45	0.83	0.73
0.15	1.02	1.56	0.64	0.15	0.16	0.65	0.83	1.46	1.43	0.26	0.62	0.30	1.40	1.07	0.72
0.2	1.03	1.60	0.67	0.25	0.30	0.56	0.97	1.64	1.45	0.22	0.63	0.37	1.07	1.38	0.69
0.25	1.33	1.17	0.71	0.31	0.42	0.89	0.76	1.64	1.02	0.23	0.61	0.22	1.02	1.42	0.79
0.3	1.18	1.15	0.57	0.31	0.43	0.77	0.80	1.60	0.68	0.26	0.35	0.22	0.98	1.90*	0.88
0.35	1.35	1.48	0.78	0.44	0.77	0.72	0.71	1.57	0.59	0.11	0.28	0.22	1.25	2.22**	0.87
0.4	0.89	1.13	0.67	0.40	0.84	0.69	0.53	1.49	0.52	0.18	0.54	0.19	1.23	2.49***	1.06
0.45	0.98	0.88	0.74	0.25	0.69	0.93	0.77	1.09	0.48	0.27	0.64	0.31	1.35	2.10**	1.45
0.5	0.91	0.99	0.76	0.34	0.75	0.81	0.56	1.00	0.50	0.30	0.36	0.33	1.47	1.90*	1.15
0.55	0.76	0.94	0.79	0.23	0.86	0.85	0.73	0.95	0.36	0.26	0.33	0.25	1.52	1.30	1.36
0.6	0.97	0.76	0.73	0.30	0.69	0.73	0.63	0.78	0.43	0.19	0.39	0.21	1.19	0.88	0.98
0.65	1.04	1.08	0.49	0.42	0.43	0.59	0.66	0.74	0.55	0.23	0.29	0.17	1.06	1.16	1.17
0.7	1.09	0.72	0.65	0.40	0.68	0.64	0.42	0.85	0.58	0.23	0.40	0.23	1.21	0.81	1.43
0.75	0.92	0.60	0.58	0.29	0.57	0.60	0.60	0.41	0.58	0.17	0.39	0.22	0.89	0.52	1.77*
0.8	0.76	0.63	0.52	0.24	0.45	0.75	0.84	0.81	0.58	0.10	0.21	0.22	0.93	0.39	1.45
0.85	0.71	0.49	0.40	0.12	0.33	0.61	0.59	0.33	0.40	0.14	0.10	0.24	0.94	0.46	0.93
0.9	0.62	0.48	0.58	0.11	0.16	0.61	0.34	0.33	0.28	0.11	0.14	0.13	0.59	0.44	0.62

Note: The asterisk indicates the rejection of the null hypothesis of non-causality at the 10% (*), 5% (**) and 1% (***) level of significance.

Table 2.8. Causality-in-mean results for Asian emerging markets

Quantiles	China			India			Indonesia			Korea			Malaysia		
	EPU	GPR	FS	EPU	GPR	FS	EPU	GPR	FS	EPU	GPR	FS	EPU	GPR	FS
0.1	1.12	0.94	0.86	0.85	0.58	0.84	1.89*	1.79*	1.55	1.34	1.25	0.89	1.54	1.65	1.47
0.15	1.67*	1.05	1.16	1.01	0.86	0.84	1.78*	1.75*	1.65*	1.49	1.69	1.35	1.90*	1.74*	1.52
0.2	1.55	1.71	1.17	0.98	1.29	1.32	1.98*	1.62	1.88**	1.58	1.74*	1.62	1.87*	1.94*	1.80*
0.25	1.53	1.61	1.45	1.04	1.51	1.11	2.50***	1.80*	2.18**	1.30	1.84*	1.94**	2.06***	1.55	1.99**
0.3	1.85*	1.56	1.25	1.13	1.25	1.24	2.51***	2.06**	2.32**	1.30	1.79*	1.83**	2.35***	1.66*	1.51
0.35	1.66*	1.57	1.35	1.25	1.21	1.24	2.48***	2.11**	2.40***	1.51	2.27**	2.15**	2.33***	1.78*	1.85*
0.4	1.62	1.75*	1.35	1.43	1.44	1.24	2.77***	2.19**	2.17**	1.50	2.93***	2.30**	1.75*	1.57	1.80*
0.45	1.89*	1.89*	1.63	1.38	1.13	1.20	2.73***	2.09**	2.27**	1.70*	3.03***	2.29**	1.71*	1.54	1.93*
0.5	1.78*	1.75*	1.75*	1.65*	1.24	1.15	2.92**	2.12**	2.11**	1.55	2.80***	2.41***	1.80*	1.54	1.83*
0.55	1.87*	1.87*	1.69*	1.42	1.23	1.15	2.72***	2.45***	1.96**	1.77*	2.88***	2.72***	1.62	1.68*	1.96**
0.6	2.14**	1.70*	1.61	1.18	1.21	1.29	2.46***	2.08**	1.79*	1.61	2.72***	2.13**	1.55	1.74*	2.07**
0.65	1.94*	1.88*	1.57	1.18	1.00	1.08	2.63***	2.06**	1.69*	1.44	2.03**	1.38	1.82*	1.72*	1.75*
0.7	1.89*	1.46	1.65*	1.20	1.23	1.34	2.44***	1.60	1.59	1.26	2.44***	1.40	1.83*	1.56	1.87*
0.75	1.42	1.40	1.31	1.24	1.11	1.90*	2.05**	1.76*	1.56	1.31	2.48***	1.44	1.86*	1.31	1.47
0.8	1.27	1.25	1.23	1.22	0.79	1.78*	1.89*	1.53	1.19	1.21	2.42***	1.24	1.75*	1.09	1.42
0.85	1.12	1.19	1.01	0.79	0.71	1.47	1.84*	1.06	0.99	1.18	1.72**	0.84	1.73*	0.90	1.06
0.9	0.82	0.54	0.55	0.47	0.60	0.57	1.34	0.75	1.20	0.82	0.87	0.72	1.23	0.74	0.74

Quantiles	Pakistan			Philippines			Taiwan			Thailand		
	EPU	GPR	FS	EPU	GPR	FS	EPU	GPR	FS	EPU	GPR	FS
0.1	1.12	0.94	0.86	0.85	0.58	0.84	1.89*	1.79*	1.55	1.34	1.25	0.89
0.15	1.67*	1.05	1.16	1.01	0.86	0.84	1.78*	1.75*	1.65*	1.49	1.69*	1.35
0.2	1.55	1.71	1.17	0.98	1.29	1.32	1.98**	1.62	1.88*	1.58	1.74*	1.62
0.25	1.53	1.61	1.45	1.04	1.51	1.11	2.50***	1.80*	2.18**	1.30	1.84*	1.94*
0.3	1.85*	1.56	1.25	1.13	1.25	1.24	2.51***	2.06**	2.32**	1.30	1.79*	1.83*
0.35	1.66*	1.57	1.35	1.25	1.21	1.24	2.48***	2.11**	2.40***	1.51	2.27**	2.15**
0.4	1.62	1.75*	1.35	1.43	1.44	1.24	2.77***	2.19**	2.17**	1.50	2.93***	2.30**
0.45	1.89*	1.89*	1.63	1.38	1.13	1.20	2.73***	2.09**	2.27**	1.70*	3.03***	2.29**
0.5	1.78*	1.75*	1.75*	1.65*	1.24	1.15	2.92***	2.12**	2.11**	1.55	2.80***	2.41**
0.55	1.87*	1.87*	1.69*	1.42	1.23	1.15	2.72***	2.45***	1.96**	1.77*	2.88***	2.72***
0.6	2.14**	1.70*	1.61	1.18	1.21	1.29	2.46***	2.08**	1.79*	1.61	2.72***	2.13**
0.65	1.94*	1.88*	1.57	1.18	1.00	1.08	2.63***	2.06**	1.69*	1.44	2.03**	1.38
0.7	1.89*	1.46	1.65*	1.20	1.23	1.34	2.44***	1.60	1.59	1.26	2.44***	1.40
0.75	1.42	1.40	1.31	1.24	1.11	1.90*	2.05**	1.76*	1.56	1.31	2.48***	1.44
0.8	1.27	1.25	1.23	1.22	0.79	1.78*	1.89*	1.53	1.19	1.21	2.42***	1.24
0.85	1.12	1.19	1.01	0.79	0.71	1.47	1.84*	1.06	0.99	1.18	1.72*	0.84
0.9	0.82	0.54	0.55	0.47	0.60	0.57	1.34	0.75	1.20	0.82	0.87	0.72

Note: The asterisk indicates the rejection of the null hypothesis of non-causality at the 10% (*), 5% (**) and 1% (***) level of significance.

Table 2.9. Causality-in-variance results for Asian emerging markets

Quantiles	China			India			Indonesia			Korea			Malaysia		
	EPU	GPR	FS	EPU	GPR	FS	EPU	GPR	FS	EPU	GPR	FS	EPU	GPR	FS
0.1	0.70	0.52	0.35	0.51	0.42	0.50	0.42	0.95	1.00	0.32	0.51	0.59	0.83	0.70	1.18
0.15	0.59	0.54	0.65	0.64	0.46	0.81	0.49	0.65	1.35	1.01	0.87	0.68	1.38	0.96	1.51
0.2	0.93	0.63	0.69	0.64	0.48	0.77	0.59	0.63	0.81	0.99	0.80	0.69	1.13	0.99	1.65*
0.25	0.76	0.66	0.83	1.06	0.54	0.97	0.66	0.49	1.50	0.92	0.86	0.52	1.11	1.31	1.46
0.3	1.07	0.56	1.40	1.34	0.70	0.48	1.30	0.76	1.36	1.12	0.96	0.50	1.23	0.95	1.32
0.35	0.80	0.69	1.00	0.94	0.84	0.83	1.26	0.58	1.44	1.00	0.58	0.57	1.38	0.96	1.46
0.4	1.03	0.78	1.35	0.76	1.02	1.17	1.39	0.63	1.16	0.66	0.75	0.58	1.66*	1.15	1.62
0.45	0.93	0.97	1.79*	1.02	0.73	1.11	1.63	0.90	0.87	0.63	0.92	0.54	1.89*	1.35	1.72*
0.5	1.11	0.91	1.34	0.72	0.72	1.31	1.32	0.67	0.59	0.70	1.17	0.53	2.34***	1.01	1.71*
0.55	0.87	1.21	0.84	0.70	0.79	1.39	1.00	0.74	0.64	0.96	1.21	0.41	2.23**	0.92	1.91*
0.6	0.91	1.07	0.78	0.80	0.56	1.57	0.92	0.99	0.51	0.97	1.66*	0.68	1.96*	0.94	1.33
0.65	0.73	0.77	0.65	1.07	0.53	1.45	0.85	0.65	0.66	0.80	1.83*	0.55	1.90*	0.90	1.11
0.7	0.67	0.71	0.73	0.73	0.60	1.15	1.07	1.29	0.62	0.73	1.55	0.56	2.01**	1.04	1.54
0.75	0.57	0.80	0.85	0.73	0.60	0.36	1.20	0.78	0.63	0.78	1.01	0.55	1.48	0.93	1.21
0.8	0.44	0.62	0.53	0.69	0.35	0.35	1.34	0.51	0.57	0.77	0.99	0.45	1.21	0.79	1.17
0.85	0.44	0.82	0.65	0.63	0.31	0.47	0.90	0.43	0.47	0.42	0.53	0.33	1.13	0.82	0.92
0.9	0.50	0.57	0.48	0.57	0.12	0.30	0.52	0.34	0.74	0.53	0.60	0.37	0.88	0.64	0.57

Quantiles	Pakistan			Philippines			Taiwan			Thailand		
	EPU	GPR	FS	EPU	GPR	FS	EPU	GPR	FS	EPU	GPR	FS
0.1	0.45	0.45	0.39	0.32	0.48	0.58	0.69	0.34	0.60	0.46	0.77	0.51
0.15	0.75	0.46	0.51	0.41	0.53	0.93	0.68	0.58	0.48	0.59	0.90	0.79
0.2	0.64	0.78	0.59	0.66	0.76	1.11	0.45	0.42	0.55	0.81	1.02	0.53
0.25	0.55	0.96	0.54	0.78	0.71	0.64	0.57	0.61	0.67	0.73	1.03	0.55
0.3	0.65	0.81	0.74	1.28	0.98	0.91	0.79	0.75	0.67	1.00	0.93	0.70
0.35	0.77	0.66	0.49	1.62	0.59	0.86	0.90	0.80	0.70	1.24	1.02	0.91
0.4	0.59	0.72	0.74	1.77*	0.69	1.01	0.85	0.72	0.58	1.08	1.07	0.69
0.45	0.60	0.82	0.77	1.84*	0.85	0.95	0.72	0.60	0.74	0.76	1.10	0.68
0.5	0.79	1.27	0.82	1.50	0.70	0.91	0.70	0.77	0.84	0.75	1.16	0.69
0.55	0.81	1.27	0.74	0.86	1.28	1.00	0.86	0.68	0.84	0.84	1.60	0.48
0.6	0.98	1.41	0.70	0.94	1.12	0.87	0.96	0.74	1.12	0.85	1.64*	0.36
0.65	0.74	1.04	0.74	0.85	1.03	0.73	0.65	0.69	1.00	0.75	1.45	0.42
0.7	0.76	0.78	0.55	0.62	0.73	0.67	0.72	0.61	1.06	0.70	1.66*	0.58
0.75	0.66	0.78	0.32	0.57	0.78	0.72	0.57	0.50	0.75	0.56	1.04	0.57
0.8	0.55	0.59	0.34	0.67	0.61	0.73	0.61	0.58	0.76	0.72	0.72	0.64
0.85	0.47	0.47	0.33	0.78	0.64	0.61	0.47	0.47	0.72	0.52	0.51	0.45
0.9	0.52	0.56	0.47	0.70	0.43	0.44	0.28	0.65	0.46	0.29	0.33	0.47

Note: The asterisk indicates the rejection of the null hypothesis of non-causality at the 10% (*), 5% (**) and 1% (***) level of significance.

CHAPTER 3

OIL PRICE SHOCKS AND EMERGING STOCK MARKETS REVISITED

This essay examines the second question, that is how the different sources of oil shocks impact the emerging stock markets of distinct oil-dependence profile across the regimes and market states. Using the Markov regime switching and quantile regression model the reports no strong evidence of regime-dependence, however, the stock returns appear to be vulnerable in the bearish market states.

3.1. Background

Oil price is one of the crucial drivers of economic growth and prosperity for the developing economies. This claim is backed by fairly sizable literature, which advocates that any economy is susceptible to oil price shocks through several transmission channels such as inflation, investor's and business confidence, increasing cost of production, output and employment, for instance see (Barsky and Kilian, 2004; Hamilton, 2003; Kilian, 2008a; Lardic and Mignon, 2008) among others. The stock markets being endogenous to the economic system, some degree of interdependence is well expected with the oil prices (Huang et al., 1996). Theoretically, oil prices can be influential to the stock market performance in multifarious ways, both negatively and positively. Such as the stock price of a particular firm at time t may be expressed as the expected present value of future discounted cash flows (Huang et al., 1996). The future cash flows to the firm is vulnerable to oil price hike both directly and indirectly. Firstly, oil price rise can lead to increased cost of productions and consequently lower profits thus reducing the future cash flows to the firm i.e. direct channel.[12] Secondly, oil price rises are often perceived inflationary by policy makers. As a counter measure to control inflationary pressures the interest rates are often raised, which in turn affects the discounting factor used in pricing the stocks i.e. indirect channel. These events are likely to have a negative impact on the stock prices. Nevertheless, oil and stock may also have a positive relationship caused by the steering demand for oil as industrial input in the phase of industrial growth. Consequently, the stock and oil prices increase simultaneously (Ciner, 2013; Kilian and Park, 2009). A vast array of recent literature validates the oil-price and stock returns relationship, for example, (Basher and Sadorsky, 2006; Boyer and Filion, 2007; Jones and Kaul, 1996; Kang and Ratti, 2013; Kang et al., 2016; Mohanty et al., 2010; Moya-Martínez et al., 2014; Nandha and Faff, 2008; Ready, 2018) among others.

This explicitly focuses upon the relationship between emerging stock markets (EM) and oil prices. The underlying reasons are manifold. As it is prevalent in the literature that the global portfolio investors seek the benefits of the international diversification by investing in EM, since EM are less correlated with developed markets and have higher return yields (Bekaert and Harvey, 1997; Grubel, 1968; Levy and Sarnat, 1970). Besides, it is now well-recognized that the era of globalization has amplified flows of financial capital, goods and services across the international borders, especially in the EM. Consequently, the cross-economy interdependencies in world trade have increased much than before. Thus, the world trade and commerce are now more exposed to oil price shocks with ushering importance of emerging economies like Brazil, India, China (Basher and Sadorsky, 2006).[13] Furthermore, it must be noted that the developed economies are more energy efficient in comparison to emerging economies with the intervention of technological innovations and optimum diversification between renewable and non-renewable sources of energy.[14] The emerging economies, on the other hand, are more energy reliant and hence the risk exposure to oil price shocks is more. We validate this claim using the energy consumption growth rate statistics over the period 2006-2016 exhibited in Figure 3.1. Figure 3.1 (a) and (b) exhibits the energy consumption growth rate for developed and emerging countries respectively. It may be easily observed that for the developed countries (G7 and others) the energy consumption has gradually resorted to a negative growth rate with only exception to Canada[15]. In the case of the emerging countries, it is clearly evident that the energy consumption has a positive growth rate with marginal exception to Greece[16], Hungary and CR. It must be considered that the emerging countries exhibit substantial growth potentials and have grown at a rapid pace. The emerging countries in our sample is the home to 58% of the world's population covering 38% of the global land area, which contributes to 34% of the world's GDP.[17] Furthermore, the world's leading investment banking houses such as Goldman Sachs expects a group of steadily growing emerging countries (Brazil, Russia, India and China) to surpass the nominal GDP of G7 nations by the year 2050. Therefore, the impending growth in GDP is expected to increase the energy demand by these nations in future. Besides, inflows capital and foreign portfolio investments may also be anticipated to rise considerably with the growth momentum of these nations. As we have discussed before, the rising energy demands is expected to expose a nation towards oil price risks. Thus, novel insights concerning the impact of oil price movements on the risk-return profile of equities in EM would enable the investors to understand the inherent risk in their portfolios.

---

[13] Author uses the terms *emerging economies/countries* and *developing economies/countries* interchangeably. Similarly, for the terms *advanced economies/countries* and *developed economies/countries*. By using the term economy, author considers the countries as the marketplace which transacts and facilitates creation of wealth.

[14] Basher and Sadorsky (2006) states that the oil consumption per dollar of Gross Domestic Product (GDP) has dropped significantly by less than half of the value of what it was in the decade of 1970. In this , we focus upon some recent statistics and show that the advanced economies mostly depict negative energy consumption growth rate over the decade 2006-2016 (*see* Figure 3.1 (a)).

[15] It must be noted that the rate of energy consumption also depends upon energy usage costs, lifestyle and geographic location or the climatic conditions. For example, some provinces in Canada such as, Alberta, British Columbia, Manitoba, Ontario, Saskatchewan have low energy prices for residential homes on a gigajoule basis. Thus, the lower costs may incentivize higher levels of energy usage. Additionally, in Canada the statistical reports reveal that more people own light trucks in Alberta, Manitoba, Saskatchewan and Newfoundland, which also drives up the energy usage. Finally, it must also be understood that the average temperature of Canada is about -15 to -20 degrees Celsius, which may drop down further during winters. Thus, the residents are required to use more energy to heat their homes for a comfortable living. (Readers are requested to access to the full article online article for further details: https://www.canadiangeographic.ca/article/energy-use-canada, accessed 10/10/2018, 19:52 Hours, IST)

It also worth mentioning that the past episodes of oil price shocks have clearly established the higher vulnerability of relatively poorer economies. For instance, the rise in oil prices from US$ 3 to US$ 13 per barrel in 1973 on account of the OPEC oil embargo led to economic hardships and severity for many of the developing nations. The skyrocketed price of oil raised the cost of oil imports hampering the rate of growth and economic development. The international lending organizations (such as the World Bank and International Monetary Fund) attempted to rescue the developing nations by availing funds for the economic development projects (Rifkin, 2003). However, such lending soon converted to mounting debt which increased by 550%. The subsequent oil price shock in 1979 worsened the situation even further leading to global recession with rising oil import prices and falling export prices of production from developing nations. Soon in 1985 the total debt volume amounted to US$ 1 trillion. The most of the developing nations were stuck by a debt vicious circle where funds were being borrowed for importing oil and interest payments on existing debts (Basher and Sadorsky, 2006). Accordingly, the residual margin of leftover funds for development projects were inadequate. Thus, the troika of oil price rise, mounting debt and sluggish economic development is a serious concern for the developing nations.[18]

In this , we examine the susceptibility of the stock markets in emerging economies. It is well recognized that stock market is the barometer and indicator of prosperity of an economy. Thus, it is imperative to understand the influence of oil price shocks on EM. Though we are not the first group of scholars to investigate this relationship, however, our differs significantly from the previous studies and offers a fresh perspective. The majority of the previous studies focusing upon the EM and oil prices such as Aloui et al., (2012), Basher and Sadorsky (2006), Basher et al., (2012), Broadstock et al., (2012), Broadstock and Filis (2014), Mensi et al., (2014), Zhu et al., (2016) among others, are constrained by some limitations.[19] These studies either overlook to incorporate the source of oil price shocks (i.e. whether the shock is demand or supply driven) or the decomposition of oil price shock is performed using the algorithm of Kilian (2009). For a holistic understanding of oil price and stock market dynamics, it is important to understand the source of shock origination to identify whether the stock markets are more sensitive to supply shocks or demand shocks. To facilitate such a purpose Kilian (2009) suggests a shock decomposition procedure of oil price changes which is widely followed in the later studies with diversified contexts. However, Ready (2018) highlights some significant deficiencies of the Kilian's (2009) shock decomposition process and suggests an alternative algorithm that presumably overcomes the existing shortcomings.[20] Hence, we use the measure of Ready (2018) to decompose the oil price shocks for the purpose of our . We find that the demand shocks are positively associated with stock markets, whereas the supply shocks are negatively related with exception to some of the oil-exporting countries. The risk-based shocks also appear to have negative association with stocks. We do not find the evidence of strong regime dependence and the direction of relationship across the high and low regimes is somewhat stable. Further, we find intense oil-stock relationship in the bearish market conditions. Alongside, we also report certain evidences of alterations of the oil-stock relationship onset the Global Financial Crisis (GFC) of 2008.

3.2. Literature review

In this section, the discusses some relevant literature closely aligned with the key objectives of our .[21] The author primarily focuses upon four diverse strands of literature in addition to the discussion of the underlying theoretical connotations of the oil-stock relationship. Theoretically, the association of oil prices with stock returns could be both positive or negative. Smyth and Narayan (2018) emphasizes that overwhelming literature can be discerned in this stream of research that attempts to scrutinize the oil-stock relationship using the cash flow hypothesis professed by Jones and Kaul (1996). The cash flow hypothesis posits that the value of a financial asset is determined by the expected future cash inflows after discounting at a certain rate (Fisher, 1930; Williams, 1938). As we have discussed earlier, oil is one of the key production inputs for most of the firms, thus higher oil price is expected to drive up cost of production. Higher production costs suppress the profit margin and choke the future stream of cash inflows to the firm which in turn affects the stock prices. Another channel of negative oil-stock relationship is higher nominal interest rates and overestimation of expected inflation rates due to rising trajectory of oil prices. Since the interest rate is used to discount the future cash inflows, higher interest rate will depress the earnings, dividends and consequently the stock returns. Alongside the negative association, a positive relationship may also be expected since the oil price rise may be attributed to the booming state of an economy Kollias et al., (2013) i.e. price rise could be demand driven. Additionally, the volatility in oil prices could drive up the risk-premium component of the stock returns which may also be ascribed to the positive oil-stock relationship. We discuss some other categorical facets of oil-stock relationship as below:

3.2.1. Oil price shocks and stock returns

Prior to the seminal work of Kilian (2009) that suggests a procedure to disentangle oil prices into demand and supply shocks, the studies mostly used the oil price changes to investigate its impact on the stock returns. Kilian and Park (2009) argue that estimates of oil-stock relationship by simply using the oil price changes may turn out to be biased since the dependence of stock returns is captured only in response to the average value of oil prices. Kilian (2009) and Kilian and Park (2009) have clearly demonstrated that the impact of oil price fluctuations on stock returns in US is distinguishable depending upon the nature, structure and source of shocks. Kilian (2009) primarily disentangles the oil price changes into three components: (a) *oil supply shocks* (unforeseen changes in petroleum production), (b) *aggregate demand shocks* (global business cycle determined oil demand) and (c) *oil-specific demand shocks* (sudden rise in oil demand as a precaution for expected future oil shortfalls). Kilian and Park (2009) acknowledges that the demand shocks (both aggregate and oil specific) are considerably imperative in explaining the US stock returns than the supply shocks. Further, they also find that the aggregate demand shock is positively related to US stock returns, however, negatively associated with oil-specific demand shocks. Regarding the supply shocks Hamilton (2009a, 2009b) also argues closely similar to Kilian and Park (2009) that supply shocks owe little stock returns predictability with changing macroeconomic dynamics. Extending the methodological framework of Kilian (2009) in an allied context, Kang et al., (2016) decomposes US and non-US based oil shocks. Kang et al., (2016) reports that positive

US supply shocks are positively associated to stock returns with increase in production onset 2009. Besides, Kang et al., (2016) also provides some contradicting results to Kilian and Park (2009) that the non-US supply shocks have similar impact as demand shocks upon the US stock returns. Furthermore, Kang et al., (2016) advocates that the stock returns predictability of aggregate demand and supply shocks are time-varying. Moreover, the aggregate demand shock emerges to be more important than the supply related shocks, consistent with Kilian and Park (2009) and Hamilton (2009a, 2009b).

Several other studies are conducted using the decomposition procedure suggested by Kilian (2009) considering different countries and stocks as examination units. The results for demand shocks is fairly consistent with Kilian (2009) among the different studies showing positive relationship with aggregate demand shocks and negative relationship with oil-specific demand shocks (Abhyankar et al., 2013; Basher et al., 2012; Filis et al., 2011; Gupta and Modise, 2013; Koh, 2017), however, the relationship of supply shock and stock returns is swerving and inconsistent across the literature. For instance, some studies find a positive association with stock returns (Abhyankar et al., 2013; Basher et al., 2018, 2012), whereas some report a negative relationship (Basher et al., 2018; Cunado and de Gracia, 2014; Gupta and Modise, 2013). Using eight developed countries as the sample set Apergis and Miller (2009) find marginal impact of supply shocks on the stock returns similar to previous studies (Hamilton, 2009a, 2009b; Kang et al., 2016; Kilian and Park, 2009). On a close note, Güntner (2014) studies the oil-stock dynamics in six countries, which are constituents of the Organization of the Economic Co-operation and Development (OECD) group. Consistent with previous studies, Güntner (2014) finds positive association with aggregate demand shocks and marginal effect of supply shocks. Nevertheless, the result varies for oil specific demand shocks in respect of the oil importing and exporting countries. Güntner (2014) reports positive relationship in the case of Norway, which is a net oil exporter. While negative effect in regards of the net oil importing countries. The impact of such oil shocks is also studied across the industrial sectors. For example, Broadstock and Filis (2014) the sectorial stock returns responses to oil price shocks are diverse and varied.

3.2.2. Time-varying nature of oil-stock relationship

The extant literature shows that the oil-stock relationship is inherently nonlinear. In other words, it has been observed that the oil prices stimulate the movements in stock returns differently for booming and recessionary periods. The theoretical and expected oil-stock relationship could often be altered or distorted by exogeneous events such as economic turbulences (financial crises), geopolitical or war-like tensions (Ajmi et al., 2014). Such as the oil-stock relationship is found unstable by Mohaddes and Pesaran (2017) in the context of US for the period spanning over 1946-2017. Certain studies also claim that the response of US stock returns to oil price shocks varied largely before, during and after the GFC, for example *see* (Mollick and Assefa, 2013; Tsai, 2015). Such empirical evidence is also reported by Miller and Ratti (2009), they contend that onwards September 1999 the long-run negative oil-stock link diminished gradually. Several other studies use diverse methodological approaches (such as Markov-switching, Markov-switching vector autoregression, wavelet-based decomposition etc.) to capture the nonlinear and time-varying feature of the relationship, *see* (Aloui and Jammazi, 2009; Broadstock and Filis, 2014; Ciner, 2013; Daskalaki and Skiadopoulos, 2011; Kang et al., 2015a, 2015b; Martin-Barragán et al., 2015; Reboredo, 2010; Reboredo et al., 2017; Reboredo and Rivera-Castro, 2014; Wang et al., 2015; Xu, 2015; Zhang, 2017; Zhang and Li, 2016; Zhu et al., 2017). The use of non-parametric panel data model has also been used to empirically demonstrate the nonlinear nature of oil-stock relationship, for instance, *see* Silvapulle et al., (2017).

Besides, the previous studies have also examined the asymmetric impact of negative and positive oil price movements at the different quantiles of the stock returns, where the quantiles essentially signify the state of the market in terms of bearish, normal and bullish, *see* (Ding et al., 2016; Lee and Zeng, 2011; Peng et al., 2017; Reboredo and Ugolini, 2016; Sim and Zhou, 2015; You et al., 2017; Zhu et al., 2016). The array of studies conforms a general consensus upon asymmetric impact of oil price shocks upon the stock returns. Additionally, the relationship is comparatively tractable and intense in the lower than upper quantiles (Peng et al., 2017; Reboredo and Ugolini, 2016; Sim and Zhou, 2015; Zhu et al., 2016, 2015). Nonetheless, the effects are not constant rather they are time and market-state dependent in addition, asymmetries could also alter on the occurrence of economic crises episodes. For instance, Reboredo and Ugolini (2016) using the sample of three developed and five EM, report that prior to the GFC, asymmetric relationship was somewhat subtle, which turned to be more assertive in the post-GFC era. The heterogeneous impact of oil price swings on stock returns across the market-states is also confirmed by Lee and Zeng (2011) for the G7 markets and Zhu et al., (2016) for the Chinese industrial sector returns.

3.2.3. Oil-stock relationship in oil-exporting and importing economies

The oil price oscillations may not impact the stock returns of the oil-exporting and importing economies alike. The oil-exporting countries are likely to benefit from the oil price rise since it will augment country's income and hence the GDP.[22] Thus, the stock returns are expected to receive positive stimulus by virtue of higher national earnings. The oil-importing countries, on the other hand, is expected have negative influence on the stock prices. Oil is a vital input in the production process thus, higher input prices may lead to thinning of profit margin and hence stock prices might depict plummeting tendencies. Ample studies in the past examine the oil-stock association considering oil-exporting and importing countries as sample units, such as (Boldanov et al., 2011; Filis et al., 2011; Park and Ratti, 2008; Ramos and Veiga, 2013; Salisu and Isah, 2017; Wang et al., 2013). Some studies have considered net oil importing countries in the sample set, *see* (Bouri, 2015; Cunado and de Gracia, 2014; Masih et al., 2011; Silvapulle et al., 2017), whereas some studies focus upon the oil-exporting countries explicitly, *see* (Arouri and Rault, 2012; Basher et al., 2018; Bjørnland, 2009; Demirer et al., 2015; Gil-Alana and Yaya, 2014; Mohanty et al., 2010; Park and Ratti, 2008; Ramos and Veiga, 2013). The overall results of these studies are fairly consistent with the theoretically expected relationship (Arouri and Rault, 2012; Bjørnland, 2009; Demirer et al., 2015; Gil-Alana and Yaya, 2014; Mohanty et al., 2010; Park and Ratti, 2008).

Likewise, some studies also disentangle the oil price change into shocks using the shock decomposition procedure suggested by Kilian (2009) and examine its impact upon the stock prices in oil-importing and exporting countries (Basher et al., 2018; Cunado and de Gracia, 2014; Filis et al., 2011; Wang et al., 2013). The results of these studies are diverging or partially conclusive. Basher et al., (2018) investigates the major oil-exporting countries using a multi-factor Markov-switching framework. Their reports a negative stock-oil supply shock relationship for most of the countries. The demand shocks, however is mostly positive for all the countries (with marginal exception of Kuwait in state 1). Cunado and de Gracia (2014) on the other hand, explicitly focusses upon the oil-importing countries and documents negative stock-oil supply shock association. Filis et al., (2011) considers both oil importing and exporting in the sample set and overall concludes that the aggregate demand shocks are positively associated with stock returns, whereas the oil-specific demand shocks evinces negative impact on the stock returns. The oil supply shocks are reported to have nominal impact on the stock returns of both oil-importing and exporting countries. Furthermore, Wang et al., (2013) argues that the impact of demand shocks is positive for both importers and exports, nonetheless the influence is comparatively profound for the exporters.

3.2.4. Oil-stock relationship in emerging economies

The studies concerning the oil-stock relationship considering sample units from the universe of emerging economies is limited in literature. Smyth and Narayan (2018) clearly emphasizes upon the dearth of studies focusing on the developing countries which are witnessing an economical transitory phase and their stock markets are at an embryonic stage, with only exception to China. In comparison to the other emerging countries, abundant literature is available that focusses upon the various aspects of the oil-stock relationship in China, *see* (Caporale et al., 2015; Ding et al., 2017; Kang and Ratti, 2015; Li et al., 2017, 2012; You et al., 2017; Zhu et al., 2016, 2015). Withstanding China, limited number of studies can also be traced for other emerging countries, such as for Central and Eastern Europe (Asteriou and Bashmakova, 2013; Mohanty et al., 2010), India (Ghosh and Kanjilal, 2016; Tiwari et al., 2018b), Russia (Bhar and Nikolova, 2010), African continent countries (Gil-Alana and Yaya, 2014; Gupta and Modise, 2013; Lin et al., 2014), BRICS country-group (Brazil, Russia, India, China and South Africa) (Dogah and Premaratne, 2018; Nasir et al., 2018), Vietnam (Narayan and Narayan, 2010). Alongside, a few multi-country studies could also be traced in this sphere of literature, *see* (Aloui et al., 2012; Basher et al., 2012; Basher and Sadorsky, 2006; Gupta, 2016; Ramos and Veiga, 2013). Nevertheless, the developing world is still deprived of sufficient empirical literature with comparison to the developed countries (Smyth and Narayan 2018).

This differs from the vast array of previous studies on several grounds. First, the prior studies either do not decompose the oil prices changes into shocks or uses the shock decomposition process suggested by Kilian (2009). Ready (2018) highlights certain shortcomings of the shock decomposition process of Kilian (2009) (which we discuss in details in the methodology section), thus, we use the novel decomposition procedure of Ready (2018). Second, we use a battery of econometric tests to unravel the time-varying as well as the asymmetric nature of oil-stock relationship across market regime and states. Third, we classify the 24 sample emerging countries on the basis of oil-dependence and focus upon their degree of sensitivity to each source of oil shocks. Thus, we believe that our is insulated of some of the limitations of past literature and hence the investors, policy makers and other stakeholders may find it useful for understanding the oil-stock dynamics in the emerging markets.

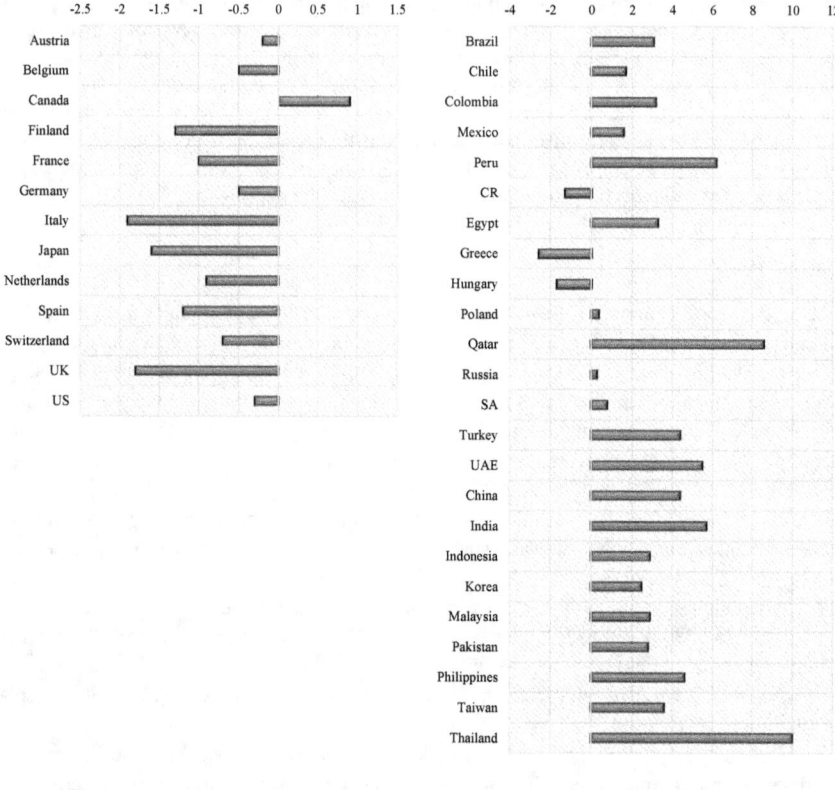

(a) G7 and other developed countries   (b) Emerging countries

Figure 3.1. Energy consumption growth rate

Notes: The figure exhibits the growth rate of energy consumption in developed and emerging countries during the period 2006 to 2016. The data is sourced from the BP Statistical Review of World Energy, June 2018. All values are expressed in percentage (%). The bars in Green (Red) color indicate positive (negative) values.
CR: Czech Republic, SA: South Africa, UAE: United Arab Emirates

3.3. Data and methodology

3.3.1. Data description

The dataset consists of 24 emerging markets as classified by the Morgan Stanley Capital International (MSCI) (Table 3.1 exhibits the classification). The considers the daily closing index prices of each market, and the data is extracted from the Bloomberg database. The Bloomberg quotes of respective markets are indicated in Table 3.1. The period of ranges from July 15, 2002 to June 18, 2018 enveloping 4013 daily observations. In order to decompose the oil price changes into the demand, supply and risk driven shocks using the procedure of Ready (2018), we consider three additional variables. The first variable is the stock price index of the oil and gas producing firms. We use the MSCI All Country World Index (ACWI) Energy Index for this purpose.[23] This is a composite index of large and midcap securities classified as the 'Energy' in the Global Industrial Classification Standard (GICS) for 23 developed and 24 emerging markets. This index covers largely publicly traded firms in oil and gas sector such as Exxon Mobil Corp (US), Chevron Corp (US), Total (FR), BP (GB), Suncor Energy (CA), Reliance Industries (IN), CNOOC (CN), LUKOIL Holding [RUB] (RU) and many others to represent the global oil industry both from the developed and emerging economies.[24] The second variable is the Chicago Board of Options Exchange (CBOE) Volatility Index (VIX), required to proxy for the changes in the market discount rates in aggregate. The changing attitudes towards the risk is assumed to potentially drive the market discount rates (Ready, 2018). The innovation in the VIX facilitates this purpose, which is estimated as the residuals of ARMA (1,1) process of the VIX. In this regard, Bollerslev et al., (2009) posit a negative correlation of variance risk premium (captivated in the VIX) with equity returns besides VIX also demonstrate reasonable predictive ability of stock returns. Thereby VIX qualify as a suitable proxy of changes in risk measure. The third variable is the oil price changes proxied by 1-month returns on NYMEX -Light Sweet Oil contracts.

Table 3.1. MSCI emerging markets classification

EMERGING MARKETS					
Americas	Index (Bloomberg Quote)	Europe, Middle East and Africa	Index (Bloomberg Quote)	Asia	Index (Bloomberg Quote)
Brazil	IBOV	Czech Republic	PX	China	SHCOMP
Chile	IPSA	Egypt	EGX30	India	SENSEX
Colombia	COLCAP	Greece	ASE	Indonesia	JCI
Mexico	MEXBOL	Hungary	BUX	Korea	KOSPI
Peru	SPBLPGPT	Poland	WIG	Malaysia	KLCI
		Qatar	DSM	Pakistan	KSE100
		Russia	MICEX	Philippines	PCOMP
		South Africa	JALSH	Taiwan	TWSE
		Turkey	XU100	Thailand	SET
		United Arab Emirates	SASEIDX		

It may be noted that the degree to which the stock returns are sensitive towards the oil price shocks is proportional to the dependency of a particular market on oil and petroleum products. Thus, it becomes both imperative and logical to subdivide the sample markets based on the oil-dependence. We must highlight the fact that our sample set is heterogeneous with

---

[23] Ready (2018) discusses the underlying conjecture for using the stock returns of the oil and gas sector firms to disentangle the changes in oil price. The stock prices of oil and gas producing firms are exposed to two contradictory nature of shocks. The first shock is 'demand pull' or the 'demand shock' i.e. the increase in oil prices due to higher oil demand and thus the oil firms are likely to benefit from the incremental sales and hence leading higher stock returns. The second shock is 'cost push' or the 'supply shock' i.e. the rise in oil prices due to incurrence of higher (input) cost in oil production. Notwithstanding, oil and gas industry inherently endow a natural hedge against any such supply shocks. The firms will sell at higher prices at the times of supply shocks, thus offsetting the impact of depressing sales. Thus, the equity prices of these firms are relatively less responsive to oil price shocks. In such a case, the stock returns of this industry can be considered as an essential variable to disentangle the oil price changes resorting from two different sources.
[24] The brackets beside the firm identities denote the location of headquarters of the respective firms mentioned as per MSCI. US: United States, FR: France, GB: Great Britain, CA: Canada, IN: India, CN: China, RU: Russia.

respect to the oil profiles, thus unarguably the oil-stock linkage is expected to vary across the markets. Several studies in the past explicitly use the bifurcation between oil-importing and exporting countries to examine the multifarious economic dimensions (Aloui et al., 2012; Basher et al., 2018; Damette and Seghir, 2013; Filis, Degiannakis, and Floros, 2011; Jiménez-Rodríguez and Sánchez, 2005; Mehrara and Oskoui, 2007; Pieschacón, 2012; Van Wijnbergen, 1984; Wang et al., 2013). Wang et al., (2013) observe that the influence of oil shocks to market returns in terms of direction, duration and even magnitude is largely determined by the status of the national economy as of oil importer or exporter in the world oil market. Additionally, the oil-dependence of a nation and its ability to influence world oil prices also govern the asymmetric exposure of a stock market towards supply or demand shocks.

The author measures the degree of oil-dependence by the aggregated volume of net exports or imports of oil in thousand barrels per day over the year 2007 to 2017. Figure 3.2 exhibits the ordering of the oil-dependence for all the markets. Based on the oil-profile ordering we classify the markets in three groups, similar to Aloui et al., (2012). Such a classification would enable us to understand the stock returns behavior of the markets with homogeneous nature of oil-dependence. The first group is termed as the *exporters*, which consists of the countries with net exports of more than 500 thousand barrels per day. The countries such as Russia, United Arab Emirates (UAE), Qatar, Mexico and Colombia fall in this group. Russia is the largest producer of crude oil in the world and its economic growth is primarily driven by energy exports. The 36% of the Russian federal budget revenues were generated by exporting the oil and natural gas products in 2016.[25] The second group is termed as the *moderate importers* with the quantum of oil imports ranging between 50 (Egypt) to 452 (Pakistan) thousand barrels per day. The 9-member countries of this group are: Egypt, Malaysia, Peru, Hungary, Czech Republic (CR), Philippines, Greece, Chile and Pakistan. We term the third group as the *importers* and comprises of 10 countries with net oil imports above 500 thousand barrels per day: South Africa (SA), Poland, Indonesia, Brazil, Turkey, Thailand, Taiwan, Korea, India and China. The countries such as China, India and Korea are among the top 10 importers of oil and gas products in the world as per the U.S. Energy Information Administration (EIA), short-term energy outlook report, May 2015.

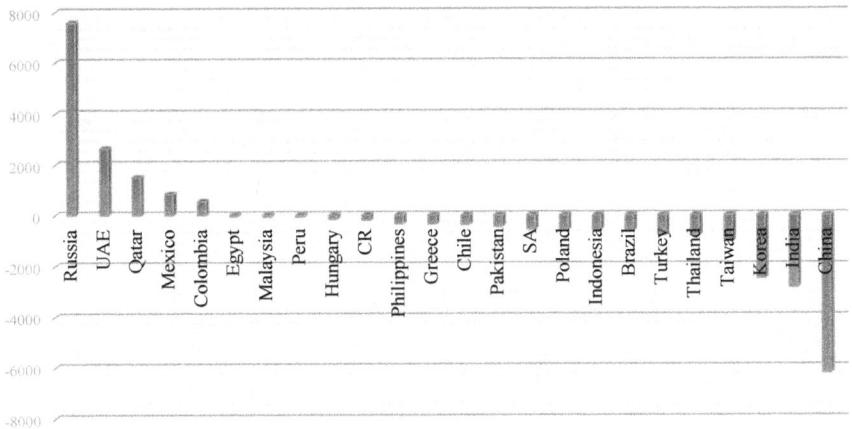

Figure 3.2. The oil-dependence profile of emerging stock markets
Notes: The figure exhibits the annual trade balance [exports (-) imports] of crude oil for the sample emerging markets during 2007 to 2017. The data is sourced from the BP Statistical Review of World Energy, June 2018. All values are expressed in '000 barrels per day.

3.3.2. Methodology

Our methodological approach is three-fold. Firstly, to decompose the oil price shocks into demand shock, supply shock and risk shock, we use the Vector Autoregression (VAR) type process suggested recently by Ready (2018). Secondly, in order to understand the regime-specific impact of decomposed oil shocks on stock returns we use the Markov regime switching (MRS) approach following the earlier literature in this domain (Aloui and Jammazi, 2009; Basher et al., 2016; Uddin et al., 2018). Lastly, to understand the nature of dependence structure between oil prices and stock returns during the full-sample period and onset the GFC, we use the bootstrapped quantile regression (QR) with presence of structural breaks following past studies (Mensi et al., 2014; Zhu et al., 2016).

3.3.2.1. The VAR model and shock decomposition

The voluminous literature investigating the relationship between oil price shocks and assets returns is plagued by two noteworthy limitations (Ready, 2018; Uddin et al., 2018). First of all, oil prices are archetypally viewed to be an exogenous variable to the economy, which may not be true since the economic system is complex and (Kilian, 2008a, 2008b). Secondly, it is crucial to identify the source of oil price shocks i.e. demand shock or supply shock. In order to address this pivotal dimension, Kilian (2009) and Kilian and Park (2009) suggested a disentangling procedure to decompose the oil price changes into demand or supply driven shocks. Several subsequent papers use this algorithm for examining the impact of oil price shocks on commodities, macroeconomic variables, financial markets and so on, for instance (Ahmadi, Behmiri, and Manera, 2016; Basher, Haug, and Sadorsky, 2012; Basher et al., 2016; Jadidzadeh and Serletis, 2017; Kim, Hammoudeh, Hyun, and Gupta, 2017; Lee, Lee, and Ning, 2017; Wang et al., 2013).

Nevertheless, Ready (2018) puts forth some of the limitations in Kilian's (2009) structural vector autoregression (SVAR) framework. Kilian (2009) uses the oil production data and shipping prices to proxy for oil supply and demand. In the subsequent work of Kilian and Park (2009) they extend the methodological approach to investigate the impact of such oil induced shocks on US stock markets. Ready (2018) highlights that Kilian and Park (2009) find very diminutive contemporaneous predictive power for stock returns, which is less than two per cent combined. Additionally, Ready (2018) also argues that the reported correlations in the work of Kilian and Park (2009) is mostly driven by the residual changes in oil prices (which is neither related to aggregated demand nor supply). The key shortcoming underlined by Ready (2018) is the fact that in Kilian and Park's (2009) algorithm, in order to effectively identify the shocks, the data (oil production, shipping prices and global economic activity) in the SVAR framework must correlate with the contemporaneous or future oil price changes. Ready (2018) further discusses that only four per cent of the contemporaneous changes in oil prices during the year 1986-2011 is explained by the identified demand and supply shocks using the SVAR framework. Of the hold out variations, 19 per cent is classified to be predictable by SVAR and the residual 77 per cent is acknowledged as the "precautionary demand shocks". Ready (2018) further emphasizes that it is difficult to ascertain whether the changes in precautionary demand is driven by the concerns over supply or the expectation of the demand changes. For instance, the oil price rise due to probable expectation of supply constraints that may not ever materialize will not be identified by using VAR. Likewise, the oil price increase due to escalated demand, which is not reflected simultaneously by increased shipping prices will also remain unidentified (Ready, 2018).[26]

To overcome the drawbacks of the SVAR procedure, Ready (2018) recently proposes a new technique to decompose the changes in oil price into demand, supply and risk shocks, which bases upon the prices of tradable assets. Specifically, the demand shocks are estimated as the contemporaneous regression residuals of global oil producing firm index returns regressed upon the innovations in the log of VIX. The supply shocks are approximated as the residue of contemporaneous changes in oil prices that is orthogonal upon the demand shocks and innovations in VIX (risk shock). In this process, the demand and supply shocks are estimated in a way that the entire variation in oil price changes is explained by demand, supply and risk shock. We follow Ready's (2018) shock decomposition procedure in this . In this process, it is assumed that demand shocks, supply shocks and risk shocks are orthogonal to each other, which may be expressed as:

$$X_t = \begin{bmatrix} \Delta op_t \\ R_t^{Oil\ Prod} \\ \xi VIX_t \end{bmatrix}, Z_t = \begin{bmatrix} ds_t \\ ss_t \\ rs_t \end{bmatrix}, A \equiv \begin{bmatrix} 1 & 1 & 1 \\ 0 & a_{22} & a_{23} \\ 0 & 0 & a_{33} \end{bmatrix} \quad (1)$$

Where the oil price change is denoted as Δop_t, $R_t^{Oil\ Prod}$ is the global oil producing firm index returns and ξVIX_t signifies innovation in the VIX. The recognized shocks are mapped in the matrix A as observable variables.

$$X_t = A Z_t \quad (2)$$

In order to impose orthogonality, the following condition is fulfilled:

---

[26] *See* Kolodzeij and Kaufmann (2014) for an in-depth discussion on the concerns with the SVAR methodological approach in this context.

$$A^{-1}\Sigma_x(A^{-1})^T = \begin{bmatrix} \sigma_{ds}^2 & 0 & 0 \\ 0 & \sigma_{ss}^2 & 0 \\ 0 & 0 & \sigma_{rs}^2 \end{bmatrix} \qquad (3)$$

The covariance matrix of the observable term X_t is denoted by Σ_x. The volatilities of the identified shocks are represented as σ_{ds}, σ_{ss} and σ_{rs}. This is the normalization procedure of the standard orthogonalization in order to define the structural shocks in the framework of SVAR. Additionally, the shocks are constrained to represent the total oil price changes rather than normalizing the volatility of shocks to one.

3.3.2.2. Markov regime switching model

We employ the MRS regression to captivate the regime shifts in the relationship between the emerging stock market returns and oil price shocks.[27] The relevance of incorporating the structural changes in analyzing the macroeconomic time-series is pivotal, since the linear models are exposed to the risk of being mis-specified (Granger, 1996; Hansen, 2001). The mis-specification is caused by the incapability of the traditional models to capture the dynamic nonlinear patterns in the time-series. The MRS model is superior to the conventional models since it can capture the asymmetry and nonlinearity in the relationship between the time-series of the macroeconomic variables. This approach enables to identify the model parameters at different regimes by allowing parameters to switch across regimes. This approach is effective particularly when the asymmetries are caused by the events that are exogenous in nature. This aspect is crucial to our since our data period corresponds to some important economic and geopolitical events that are crucial for oil price and stock market fluctuations such as war in Iraq (2003), GFC (2008-09), European sovereign debt crisis (2009). These events are considered as exogenous macroeconomic shocks that trigger the switch in regime in a Markovian framework.[28]

Prior to the application of the MRS model, we estimate the following baseline linear regression specification to understand the relationship between the individual stock markets and oil price changes. The model is specified as below:

$$\Delta ret_{i,t} = \beta_{0,i} + \beta_{1,i}\Delta op_t + \mu_{i,t} \qquad (4)$$

where, $\Delta ret_{i,t}$ represent the logarithmic returns of the stock prices. Δop_t denotes the oil price changes and $\mu_{i,t}$ is the random error term. In the next step we disentangle the oil price changes into the shocks (demand, supply and risk shocks) as the explanatory variables. The model is specified as below:

$$\Delta ret_{i,t} = \beta_{0,i} + \beta_{1,i}ds_t + \beta_{2,i}ss_t + \beta_{3,i}rs_t + \mu_{i,t} \qquad (5)$$

where, the notations ds_t, ss_t and rs_t denotes the demand, supply and risk shocks respectively. The rationale behind reiterating the equation (4) by disentangling the oil price shocks in

---

[27] The univariate MRS autoregressive models were initially introduced by Hamilton (1990). Later on Krolzig (1997, 1999) extended this methodology for multiple time-series.
[28] MRS is a widely used model in the domain of finance and economics literature. For example, Hamilton (1989, 1990), Gray (1996), Gelman and Wilfling (2009), Aloui and Jammazi (2009), Liu et al., (2012), Balcilar and Ozdemir (2013), Eichler and Tuerk (2013), Balcilar et al., (2015), Basher et al., (2016), Philip and Shi (2016), Uddin et al., (2018).

equation (5) is to facilitate a comparison of the explanatory power between the univariate and shock decomposed multivariate model. A higher predictive ability of the shock-based multivariate model will validate the pertinence of the shock decomposition over the use composite oil price changes as explanatory variables Uddin et al., (2018). In the subsequent step, we estimate the MRS regression model using the following specification:

$$\Delta ret_{i,t} = \beta_{0,i,\ r_t} + \beta_{1,i,\ r_t} ds_t + \beta_{2,i,\ r_t} ss_t + \beta_{3,i,\ r_t} rs_t + \mu_{i,t} \qquad (6)$$

where, the r_t is a discrete regime variable and the regime dependent intercept is noted as $\beta_{0,i,\ r_t}$. The slope coefficients are represented as $\beta_{1,i,\ r_t} ds_t \ldots \ldots \beta_{3,i,\ r_t} rs_t$. We consider that the impact of oil price shocks on the stock returns is likely to be regime dependent. At time period t, the transmission probability from regime 1 to regime m at time period $t+1$ depends upon the regime at time period t entirely.[29] It is also assumed that the stochastic switching process in regime follows ergodic, homogeneous and Markov chain of first order with constant transition probabilities and finite number of regimes (M).

$$p_{lm} = P(r_{t+1} = m | r_{t+1} = l), p_{lm} \geq 0, \sum_{m=1}^{M} P_{lm} = 1 \qquad (7)$$

In order to derive the regime-dependent coefficients, we estimate the equation (6) in two regimes. In addition, two distribution assumption of error terms are considered for estimating the MRS model, the distributions are: (a) normal distribution and (b) t-distribution following Basher et al., (2016) and Uddin et al., (2018). As the Markov chain is unobservable, the estimation output includes the state probabilities. The MRS model holds a good-fit if the derived smoothed probabilities tend closer to either zero or one. We further estimate the regime classification measure (RCM) proposed by Ang and Bekaert (2002). The RCM is an indicator of the accuracy of the MRS models.

$$RCM(r) = 100r^2 (1/T) \sum_{t=1}^{T} \prod_{i=1}^{r} \hat{p}_{j,t} \qquad (8)$$

where, the RCM is the mean value of the product of p, which denotes the smoothed probabilities and the number of states (or regimes) is represented by r. The value of the RCM statistic ranges over 0 to 100. The value 0 indicates a perfect regime classification, whereas 100 signifies a detection failure of any regime classification by the MRS model. Thus, a lower value of RCM statistic is desirable.

3.3.2.3. Bootstrapped quantile regression with presence of structural breaks

Lastly, we also explore the likelihood of variations in the oil price shocks and stock returns relationship across the distribution of returns. Thus, we resort to the QR approach to address this issue. Using the QR approach we are able to recognize whether the impact of oil price shocks is consistent over the bearish and bullish market states. This methodological approach is introduced by Koenker and Bassett (1978) and is widely used to unravel the dependence structure between the financial and economic variables (Bassett and Chen, 2002; Baur, 2013; Baur et al., 2012; Baur and Schulze, 2005; Chuang et al., 2009; Das et al., 2018a; Guo et al.,

---

[29] It must be noted that the Markov switching is conditionally linear within each regime. Additionally, the switching process within the regimes is inherently stochastic. The condition of stochasticity for the switching in regime is based on a transition probability matrix (TPM) which is time-varying. The TPM in our model changes depending upon the values of intercept and the oil price shocks.

2018; Lin, 2013; Meligkotsidou, Vrontos, and Vrontos, 2009; Mensi et al., 2014; Tiwari et al., 2018; Tsai, 2012; Xiao et al., 2018; You et al., 2017; Zhu et al., 2016). Koenker (2004) advocates that QR can provide more accurate estimates than the ordinary least square (OLS) since it is less susceptible to the outliers when the underlying time-series depart from the condition of normality. As we show later that our dataset under consideration is non-normal and leptokurtic, the choice of QR is supported to discover the relationship in the extreme market conditions (i.e. bearish and bullish market states).

Nevertheless, while understanding the relationship in a QR framework we duly consider the role of the structural break which may have considerable influence over the economic relationships. Zhu et al., (2016) argues the macroeconomic catastrophic events such as financial crisis must be considered while modeling the relationship between oil price and stock returns. The role of financial crises in permanently altering the economic relationships in terms of structure and degree of dependence is well-recognized in the past literature (Das et al., 2018b; Hu, 2006; Zhang et al., 2013). Therefore, we duly consider the potential impact of GFC (2008-09) to model the relationship between the oil price shocks and the stock returns. The determination of the turning point (or the point of structural change) however, becomes crucial here. The studies in past consider diverse starting dates for dating GFC, for instance, see (Ahmad et al., 2013; Dimitriou et al., 2013; Hammoudeh et al., 2013; Reboredo, 2012; Samarakoon, 2011; Xu and Hamori, 2012). For the purpose of dating starting point of GFC, we purposefully resort to price behavior of crude oil (similar to Mensi et al., (2014)), which is logical given the context of the . It may be noted that the oil prices surged significantly in July 2008 to a record high price of 145 USD. Nonetheless, as the GFC intensified the prices declined monotonically starting from mid of July and plummeted to nearly 30 USD in December 2008, after which they tended to rise again. Thus, we establish the pre-crisis break when the prices prevailed at the peak point in the mid of July 2008 (15 July, 2008). This break date is also supported by the U.S. economic policy uncertainty index of Baker et al., (2016), which shot up shortly in August 2008.

As it is discussed earlier, the QR is relatively robust to OLS estimators in the presence of outliers, skewness and heterogeneity in the response variable (Koenker and Hallock, 2001). Let us consider y to be the dependent variable which is linearly dependent on the variable x. In such a case, the τth conditional quantile of y may be expressed as:

$$Q_y(\tau|x) = \sum_k \beta_k(\tau) x_k = x'\beta(\tau) \qquad (9)$$

where, the dynamic dependence relationship between the τth conditional quantile of y and the vector of x is given by the QR coefficient $\beta(\tau)$. The dependence is held to be conditional if the exogeneous variables are added to x, and unconditional otherwise. The complete dependence structure of y is determined by the values of $\beta(\tau)$ for $\tau \in [0,1]$. Thus, on the basis of the specific explanatory variable contained in the vector of x, there could be four prime nature of dependence structure: (a) $\beta(\tau)$ decreases (increases) corresponding to the values of τ (i.e. monotonic), (b) $\beta(\tau)$ is unchanged at different values of τ (i.e. constant), (c) $\beta(\tau)$ is similar at higher and lower quantiles (i.e. symmetric) and (d) $\beta(\tau)$ is dissimilar at higher and lower quantiles (i.e. asymmetric).

For a given τ, the coefficients $\beta(\tau)$ are estimated by a minimization process of the weighted absolute deviations between y and x, which is expressed as:

$$\hat{\beta}(\tau) = \arg\min \sum_{t=1}^{T} \left(\tau - 1_{\{y_t < x_t'\beta(\tau)\}}\right) |y_t - x_t'\beta(\tau)| \tag{10}$$

where, the indicator function is expressed as $1_{\{y_t < x_t'\beta(\tau)\}}$. The solution to the minimization problem stated above is achieved by using the linear programming algorithm proposed by Koenker and D'Orey (1987). We use the pair bootstrapping procedure suggested by Buchinsky (1995) to obtain the standard errors of the estimated coefficients. The derived standard errors are asymptotically valid under the conditions of misspecification and heteroscedasticity of the QR function.

We specify the following QR model to investigate the heterogeneous impact of conditioning variables (i.e. the oil price shocks) before and onset the GFC on the quantile function of stock returns as:

$$Q_y(\tau|x) = \alpha(\tau) + \sum_k \beta_k(\tau) x_k + D_k \left[\gamma(\tau) + \sum_k \delta_k(\tau) x_k\right] \tag{11}$$

where, $x_k = ds_t$, ss_t and rs_t. The financial crisis dummy variable is indicated by D_k. The crisis dummy takes the value of 1 onset the crisis date or 0 otherwise. The additive marginal effects of the oil price shocks onset the GFC for each τ is captured by the parameters $\gamma(\tau)$ and $\delta_k(\tau)$, which may be compared with the parameters for non-crisis sub-periods $\alpha(\tau)$ and $\beta_k(\tau)$. Baur (2013) posits that estimates from a model that do not consider D_k is biased since the dependence is completely captured by $\beta_k(\tau)$ if the dependence structure is altered by crisis. Our results clearly indicate that the dependence structure is altered by crisis, which also confirms the findings of the prior studies (Broadstock et al., 2012; Moya-Martínez et al., 2014; Zhu et al., 2016). Thus, the specified QR model allows us to scrutinize: (a) the nature of existent dependence structure between oil price shocks and stock returns; (b) how the different regressors affect the dependence structure; and (c) how the dependence structure and co-movement is affected by the GFC.

3.4. Empirical Results

3.4.1. Descriptive statistics and time-trends

Figure 3.3 exhibit trends in the time-series for the oil price, oil producer index, volatility index and the composite EM index[30]. It may be clearly observed that the slope of oil price, oil producer index and the EM index is increasing and monotonous since the beginning of 2002 till early 2008. In July 2008 on the edge of GFC, a steep fall is observed for all three variables corresponding with an abrupt spike in the VIX, which is unprecedented. Since then, the oil price, oil producer index and the EM index has recovered with relatively lower degrees of fluctuations until 2015. Another sharp fall is witnessed around October 2015 till early 2016 for the oil price and oil producer index[31]. Nonetheless, the decreasing (increasing) intensity for

---

[30] The composite MSCI index for EM is presented to exhibit the overall time-trend instead to 24 EM individually to save space.
[31] Kenneth Rogoff states that such a stunning fall in oil prices from US$ 115 in June 2014 to US$ 35 in February 2016 can be attributed to the slowing growth in the EM, particularly of the major oil importing countries such as

EM (VIX) is not as sharp as in 2008. In the upcoming years, the oil price, oil producer index and the EM index started rising persistently at a slower rate.

We show the co-movement between the oil price changes and stock returns of the EM in Figure 3.4 and 3.5 using the fixed-window rolling correlations (RC) and dynamic conditional correlations (DCC) using the bivariate DCC-GARCH (1,1) model (Engle, 2002) respectively as a preliminary analysis.[32] We perform both the analyses since Forbes and Rigobon (2002) posit that an upward bias may be exhibited in correlation coefficients, especially, for the periods corresponding to economic downturns. Forbes and Rigobon (2002) further adds that higher correlations are mainly driven by the heteroskedasticity in stock returns. After controlling for the heteroskedasticity, no convincing evidence of strong correlations is observed. In order to account for the heteroskedasticity, Akhtaruzzaman et al., (2014) suggests the use of DCC-GARCH (1,1) model. Nevertheless, Adams et al., (2017) reports the evidence that in the presence of structural breaks in the time-series of correlations the estimates of DCC-GARCH (1,1) could be spurious and hence the window rolling correlations could serve as a better alternative for the applications in empirical finance. We use both of these measures (RC and DCC) complementarily.

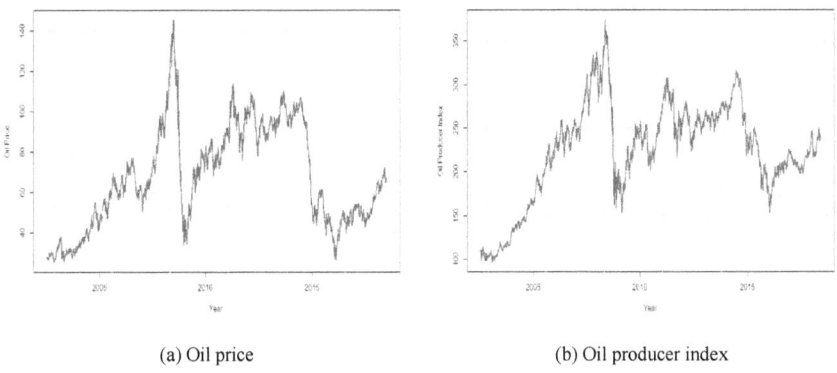

(a) Oil price　　　　　　　　　　　(b) Oil producer index

China. The full article is available at: https://www.weforum.org/agenda/2016/03/what-s-behind-the-drop-in-oil-prices/, accessed 16/10/2018, 10:18 Hours, IST. Besides, the underlying reasons for reaching oil price lows are also ascribed to the 12-year historical strong value of US$ against €. The global commodities are denominated in US$, as a result when US$ becomes stronger the value of the commodity falls i.e. more units of a commodity can be procured at a given amount of money. Additionally, the oversupply of the crude oil has also been a crucial determinant for imposing downward price pressures. The Organization of the Petroleum Exporting Countries (OPEC) decided to curb down the production in a meeting in Vienna in 2014. Among the OPEC members, Algeria, Iran and Venezuela agreed upon cutting down productions for price recoveries. However, Saudi Arabia, UAE and Gulf allies refused to the proposal. Consequently, by September 2015 the crude oil futures started to decline by virtue of global oversupply and increasing oil stockpiling.

[32] The author uses the RC and DCC analysis for the purpose of preliminary inspection of co-movement. Thus, we do not discuss about DCC-GARCH (1,1) method in the methodology section. The interested readers may refer to Vacha and Barunik (2012), Lehkonen and Heimonen (2014) among others.

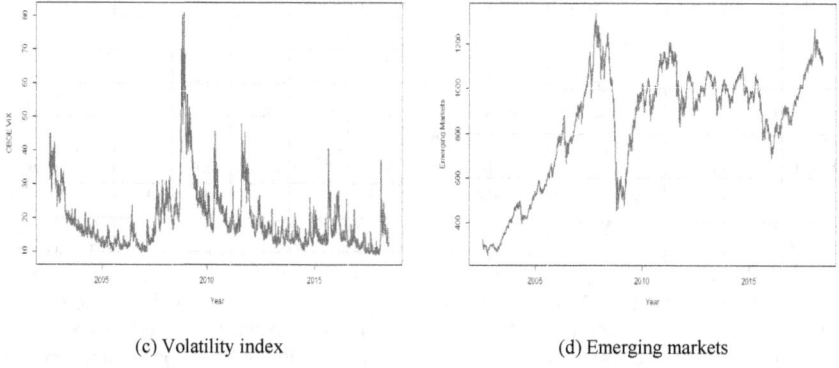

(c) Volatility index   (d) Emerging markets

Figure 3. 3. Time-trends of oil price, oil producer index, volatility index and emerging markets
Notes: All prices are represented in US$. Oil prices: 1 month returns of NYMEX -Light sweet oil contracts, Oil producers index: MSCI All Country World Index Energy, Volatility index: Chicago Board Options Exchange Volatility index, Emerging markets: MSCI Emerging markets. All data are extracted from Bloomberg.

The RC analysis clearly indicates that the relationship is time-varying and the correlation oscillates from lows to highs and positive to negative and vice-versa. The degree of correlation ranges between ±0.5 for most of the countries with exception for some of the countries during the periods of economic turbulences. Among the *exporters*, Colombia, Mexico and Russia depict a similar correlation pattern. The growth in correlation is observed since 2002 till early 2007 followed by a downturn around the period of GFC. Another price fall is observed around the end of 2014 and early 2015. The correlation increases soon after this period and falls again by late 2017-early 2018. The other two exporters, Qatar and UAE, exhibit similar co-movements, however, the correlation coefficient oscillations are subtle and somewhat within the range of ±0.5, with no exceedances. Among the moderate importers Chile, Peru, CR and Hungary exhibit correlation swings similar to the Colombia, Mexico and Russia. Whereas, the correlation series for Egypt, Greece, Malaysia, Philippines and Pakistan is relatively stable. Similarly, among the *importers*, Brazil, Poland, SA and Turkey exhibit stronger oscillations as compared to the other countries in the group. We primarily observe two important points here, first, for most of the countries the correlations increase before the major break of 2008. Additionally, the frequency of positive correlation coefficients exceeds negative ones. The RC results supports the conjecture of Kilian and Park (2009), which claims positive oil price-stock returns correlation in the beginning of the business cycle. It essentially signifies an increased demand for industrial input commodities such as oil, at the juncture of industrial growth driving up both stock returns and oil prices. Ciner (2013) also provides the evidence of positive and persistent correlations between oil and stocks. Second, it may also be noticed that the countries within the groups (as per oil-dependence profile) exhibit heterogeneous behavior of co-movement, for instance, some show rapid oscillating tendencies and some are relatively stable. Figure 3.5 presents the DCC results and it may be clearly observed that the DCC output closely corresponds with the RC analysis.[33] Thus, it is clearly evident that during the period of our the oil-stock correlation switches within the periods of high and low correlation and it is not constant in nature. Hence, we resort to the MRS approach to capture the nonlinear and asymmetric behavior since the traditional linear regression techniques fail to captivate such dynamics of the relationship (Hansen, 2001).

The summary statistics is presented in Panel A and correlation coefficients in among the oil price and its decomposed constituents Panel B of Table 3.2. The mean value for the demand shock is weak and positive. Whereas the mean value for supply and risk shock is negative for the period of our . The skewness coefficient of demand shock is negative. On the contrary, the supply and risk shock are positively skewed. Additionally, we also find that the all the three series of oil shocks exhibit the phenomenon of excess kurtosis i.e. leptokurtic with fat tails. Among the EM, the highest mean returns are observed for Egypt and the lowest mean returns (negative) are observed for Greece. The highest volatile market in terms of the standard deviation is Russia and most tranquil is Malaysia. The market returns are negatively skewed in all the cases. The negative skewness coefficients signify more frequent occurrences of negative values than the positive ones. Further we also observe the presence of positive excess value of Kurtosis coefficients which means the distributions are leptokurtotic. Nonetheless, the positive excessive Kurtosis is often preferred by the investors since it implies a higher probability of positive returns (Arouri et al., 2010). We fail to accept the null hypothesis of normality at 1% level for all the cases as shown by the J-B test.

In Panel B we report the correlation dynamics between the oil price change and decomposed oil shocks. The correlation among the shocks is insignificant and 0, which is in congruence with Ready (2018) and Uddin et al., (2018). Higher degree of correlation is observed between supply shock and oil price change, which is 0.823. It is again consistent Ready (2018) and Uddin et al., (2018) who also finds the correlation coefficient as 0.880 and 0.924 respectively. The dynamics of correlation among the EM is presented in Figure 6 in the form of a self-explanatory heat map.

We report the unit root properties of the price shocks and stock returns in Table 3.3. Two distinct as well as complementary versions of the unit root test are used. We first use the Dickey Fuller-Generalized Least Square (DF-GLS) test proposed by Elliot et al., (1996), which tests the null hypothesis of the unit root. Kwiatkowski–Phillips–Schmidt–Shin (KPSS) test (Kwiatkowski et al., 1992) on the other hand tests for the stationarity. We use the Akaike Information Criteria (AIC) as the basis for the selection of the optimum lag length. We consider both constant and trend components to conduct the test for the unit root and stationarity. The results for DF-GLS clearly shows that the null hypothesis of unit root is rejected at the 1% level of significance. Thus, the series of oil-shocks and stock returns are stationary considering the either case of constant and trend. Conversely, for the KPSS test the null hypothesis of stationarity could not be rejected. Therefore, all the series under consideration are stationary. The characteristic features of the unit root test for the disentangled oil shock series are consistent with Uddin et al., (2018).

---

[33] The parameter estimates of the DCC-GARCH (1,1) model is exhibited in the Table 3.8 below.

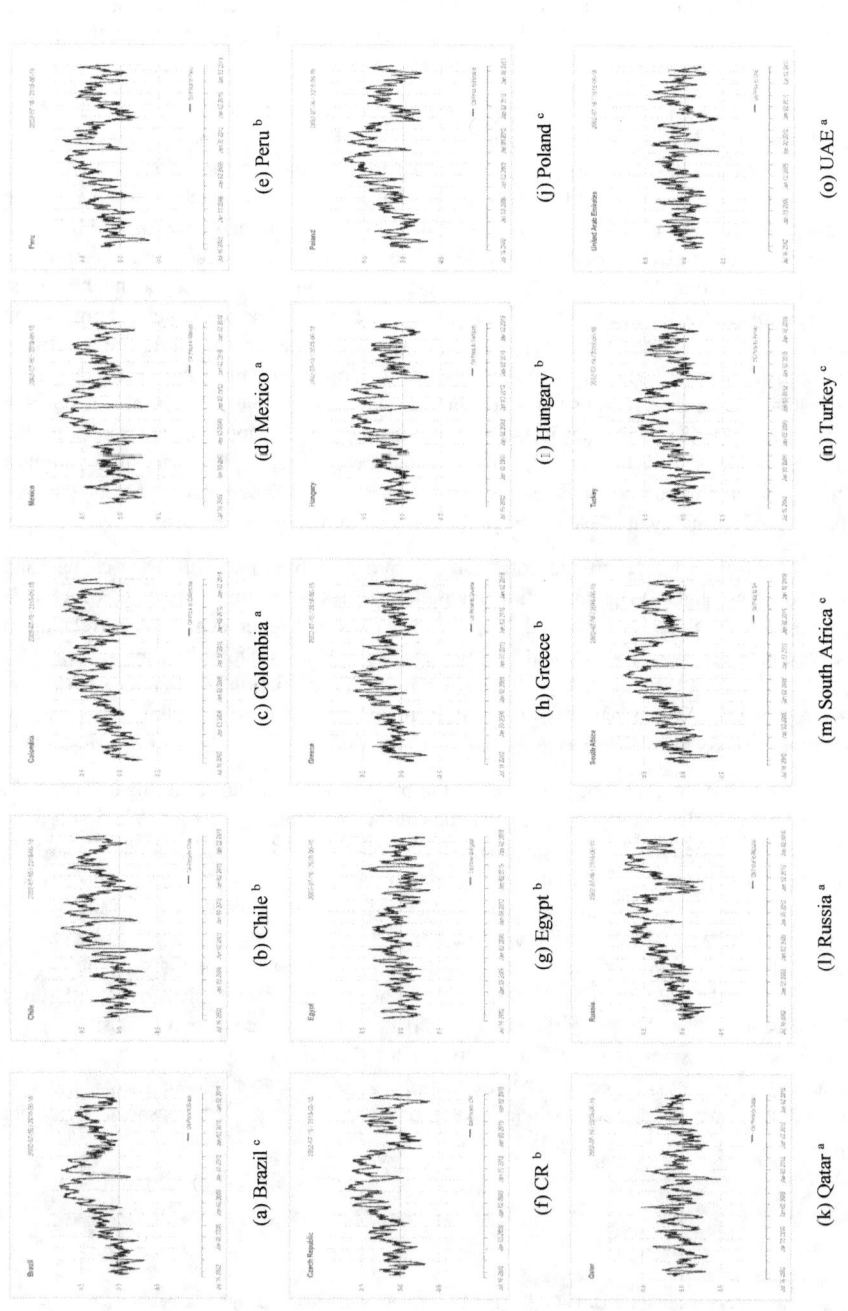

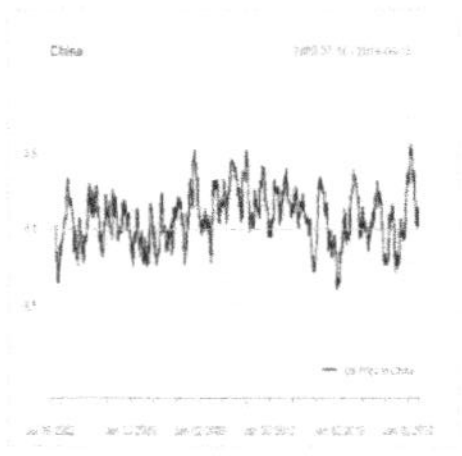

(p) China [c] 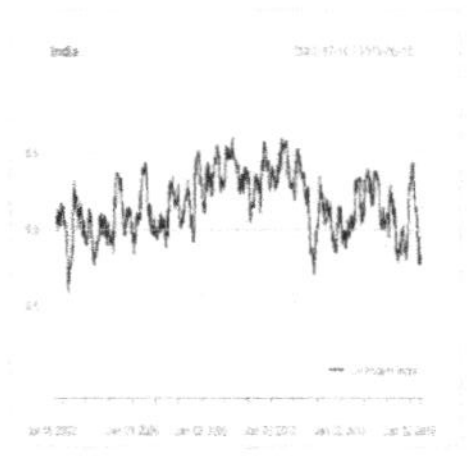　(q) India [c] 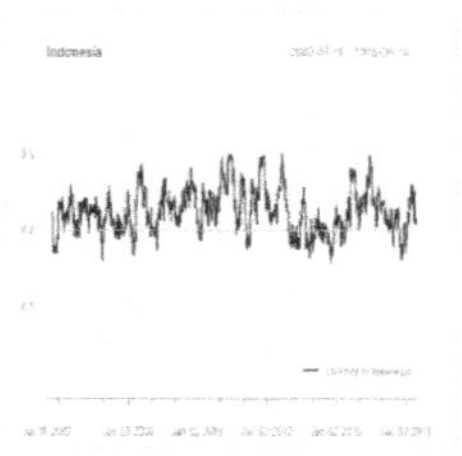　(r) Indonesia [c] 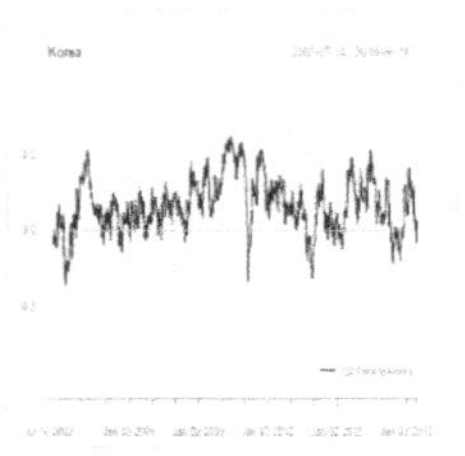　(s) Korea [c] 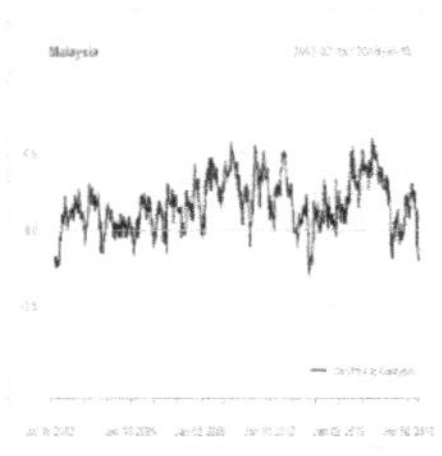　(t) Malaysia [b]

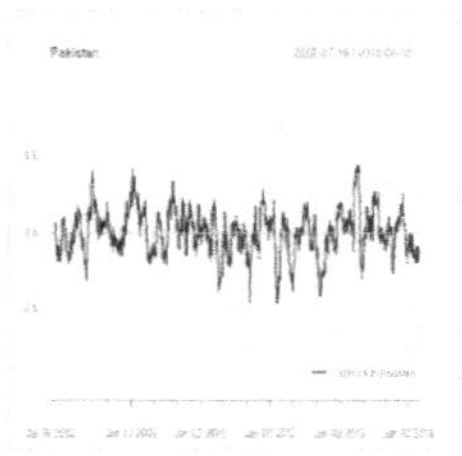

(u) Pakistan [b] 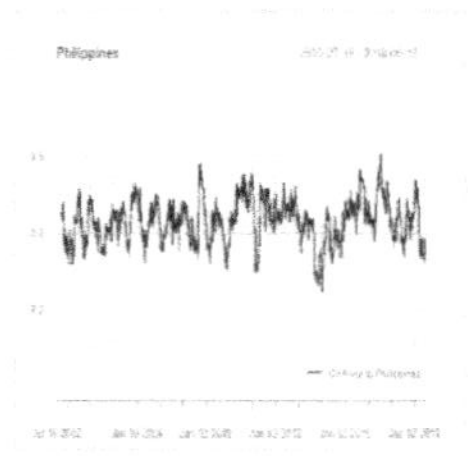　(v) Philippines [b] 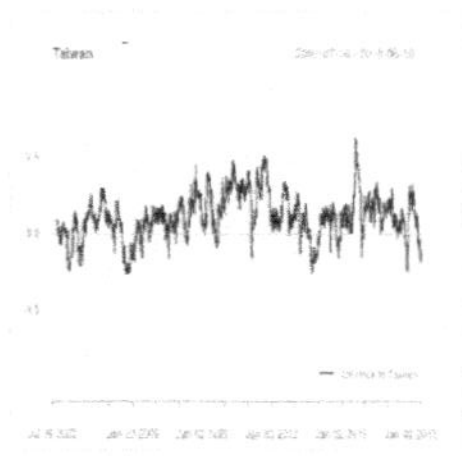　(w) Taiwan [c] 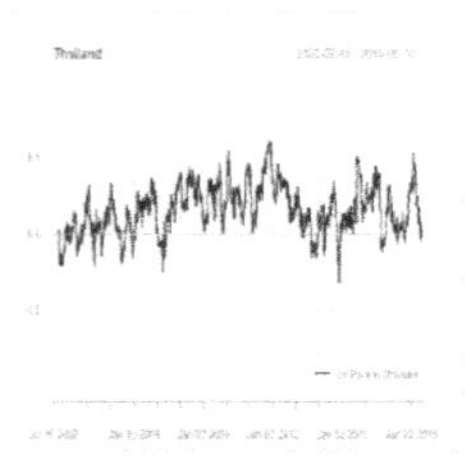　(x) Thailand [c]

Figure 3.4. Fixed-window rolling correlation
Notes: This figure exhibits the 60-period fixed-window rolling correlation between oil prices and stock returns.
[a]- Exporters, [b]- Moderate importers and [c]- Importers

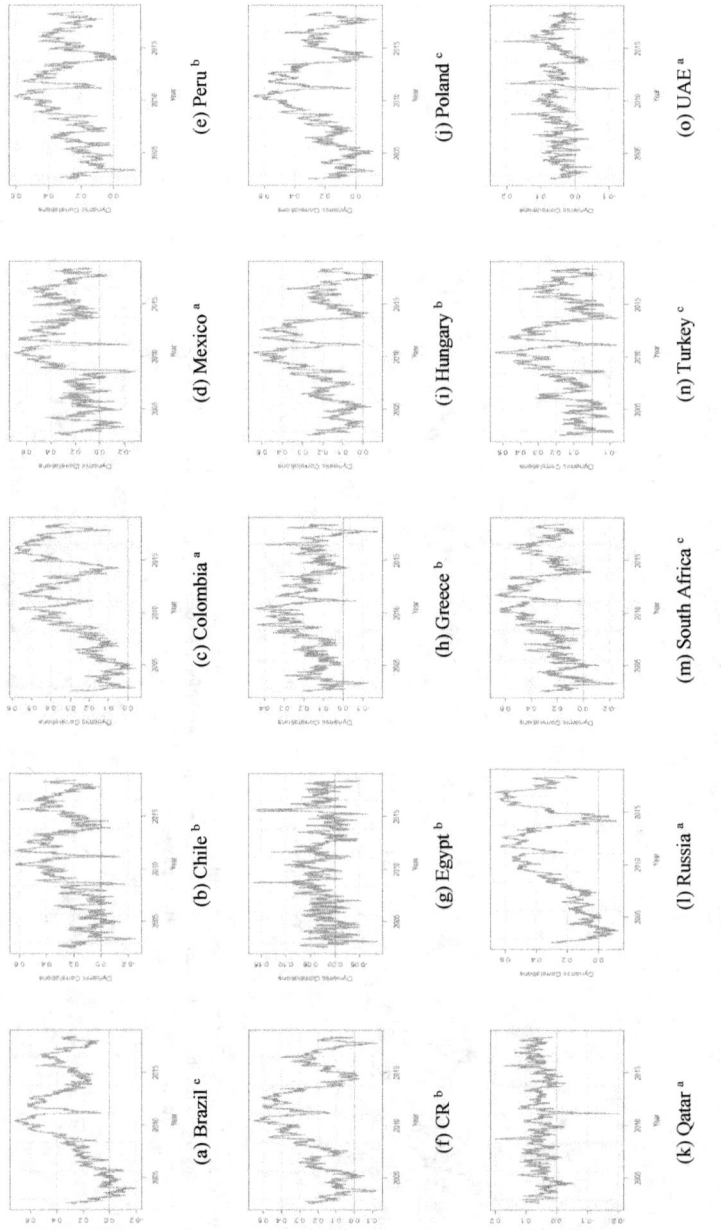

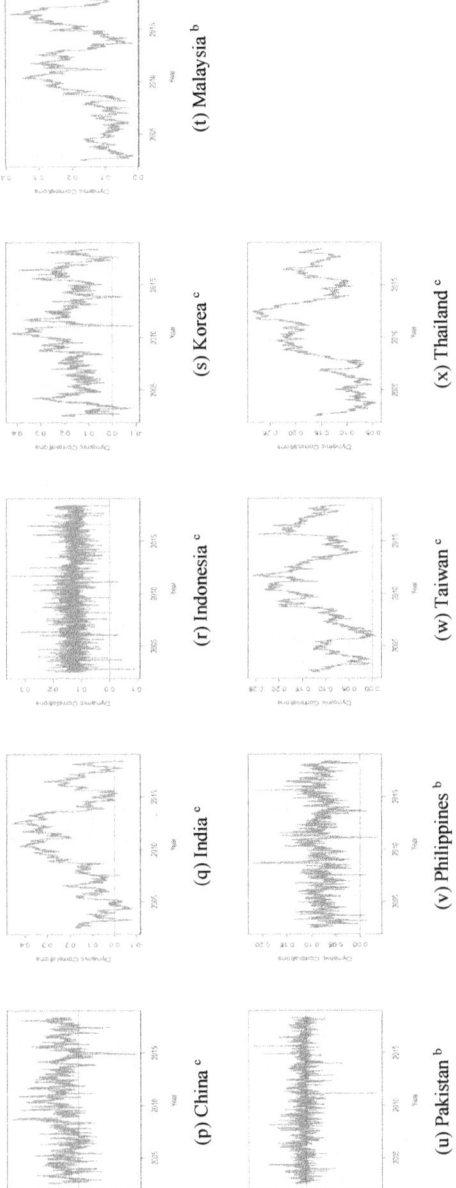

Figure 3.5. Dynamic conditional correlation

Notes: This figure exhibits the bivariate DCC using model DCC-GARCH (1,1) between oil prices and stock returns.
[a]- Exporters, [b]- Moderate importers and [c]- Importers

Table 3.2. Summary statistics and correlation coefficients

Panel A: summary statistics

	Mean	Std. Dev.	Skewness	Kurtosis	J-B
Demand shocks	0.0011	1.1978	-0.1164	11.2881	11495.00***
Supply Shocks	-0.1450	1.9175	0.2657	9.8960	7998.90***
Risk Shocks	-0.0286	6.9601	1.1576	11.0492	11729.00***
Brazil	0.0404	0.0236	-0.2702	8.7212	5521.90***
Chile	0.0453	0.0130	-0.2219	12.4026	14816.00***
Colombia	0.0558	0.0161	-0.2665	14.8398	23487.00***
Mexico	0.0310	0.0157	-0.1730	10.3178	8974.00***
Peru	0.0766	0.0150	-0.3330	14.3874	21757.00***
CR	0.0314	0.0167	-0.3452	18.4607	40048.00***
Egypt	0.1023	0.0186	-3.2835	66.2542	676230.00***
Greece	-0.0220	0.0203	-0.4308	9.8864	8053.60***
Hungary	0.0363	0.0200	-0.1546	11.0214	10775.00***
Poland	0.0385	0.0173	-0.5375	10.6329	9935.00***
Qatar	0.0392	0.0144	-0.8179	18.0358	38249.00***
Russia	0.0332	0.0240	-0.3265	17.6696	36054.00***
SA	0.0381	0.0176	-0.3112	8.3869	4916.90***
Turkey	0.0249	0.0236	-0.3044	8.7364	5564.20***
UAE	0.0423	0.0158	-1.5815	26.1532	91308.00***
China	0.0208	0.0158	-0.5703	8.7425	5731.50***
India	0.0511	0.0162	-0.1195	13.1771	17328.00***
Indonesia	0.0570	0.0163	-0.8317	14.1853	21382.00***
Korea	0.0291	0.0171	-0.5163	18.5285	40498.00***
Malaysia	0.0207	0.0092	-0.5647	11.5422	12414.00***
Pakistan	0.0668	0.0124	-0.4560	6.9490	2746.50***
Philippines	0.0446	0.0134	-0.6184	10.0144	8482.80***
Taiwan	0.0221	0.0132	-0.3196	6.8855	2592.70***
Thailand	0.0413	0.0133	-0.8024	13.8901	20260.00***

Panel B: correlation coefficients between the oil price shocks and the changes in oil price

		Δop_t	ds_t	ss_t	rs_t
Oil price change	Δop_t	1			
Demand shocks	ds_t	0.530***	1		
		(39.555)			
Supply shocks	ss_t	0.823***	0.000	1	
		(91.906)	(-0.000)#		
Risk shocks	rs_t	-0.203***	0.000	0.000	1
		(-13.153)	(-0.000)#	(-0.000)#	

Notes: The J-B, in Panel A is the abbreviation for the Jarque-Bera test of normality. The values in Panel B represents the Pearson correlation coefficient. The values of the *t*-statistics are represented in the parenthesis. # Only first three values of the *t*-statistics are reported. *** denote significance at 1% level.

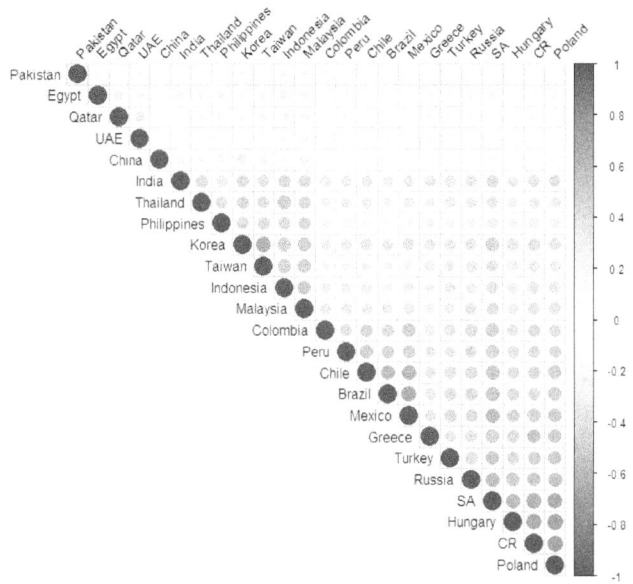

Figure 3.6. Correlation plot of stock returns
Notes: This figure exhibits the correlation among the stock returns of different markets. The color bar on the right indicates the strength of the bivariate correlation coefficient.

We further examine the stock returns distributional pattern by employing a portmanteau test i.e., Broock-Dechert-Scheinkman and LeBaron (BDS) test suggested by Broock et al., (1996). This is a widely preferred econometric technique to check the nonlinear structure and existence of spatial dependence in a time-series. In addition, the test also detects whether the time-series under consideration is independently and identically distributed (*iid*). We report the results in Table 3.4. We clearly observe that for all combinations of close point epsilon values (ε) and the embedding dimensions (m), the null hypothesis of *iid* is rejected at 1% significance level. The ε denotes the measure of *iid* residuals estimated based upon the distance of selected point pairs. Whereas, the number of consecutive points employed in the set is represented by m. Thus, overall the BDS test results indicates a possible existence of a nonlinear structure of the stock returns.

Table 3.3. Unit root tests on oil price shocks and stock market returns

	DF-GLS		KPSS	
	Constant	Trend	Constant	Trend
Demand Shock	-17.806***	-17.105***	0.564	0.038
Supply Shock	-2.831***	-5.528***	0.029	0.028
Risk Shock	-5.114***	-9.561***	0.445	0.248
Brazil	-10.069***	-13.034***	0.445	0.060
Chile	-8.649***	-11.999***	0.409	0.078
Colombia	-14.218***	-15.756***	0.916	0.072
Mexico	-14.243***	-15.614***	0.380	0.034

Peru	-9.743***	-13.991***	0.844	0.129
CR	-12.493***	-14.353***	0.490	0.141
Egypt	-7.262***	-10.847***	0.751	0.151
Greece	-7.676***	-11.595***	0.230	0.144
Hungary	-13.336***	-14.375***	0.174	0.100
Poland	-5.735***	-10.074***	0.337	0.085
Qatar	-10.577***	-13.541***	0.387	0.091
Russia	-8.514***	-12.532***	0.335	0.051
SA	-13.994***	-13.949***	0.246	0.037
Turkey	-8.656***	-13.481***	0.394	0.043
UAE	-14.743***	-15.637***	0.541	0.213
China	-14.823***	-15.782***	0.101	0.089
India	-4.878***	-8.449***	0.246	0.066
Indonesia	-14.366***	-14.818***	0.320	0.042
Korea	-6.226***	-10.077***	0.073	0.041
Malaysia	-6.688***	-9.991***	0.218	0.067
Pakistan	-4.170***	-7.946***	0.457	0.236
Philippines	-16.666***	-14.517***	0.187	0.064
Taiwan	-4.781***	-8.550***	0.033	0.034
Thailand	-5.984***	-9.217***	0.089	0.051

Notes: The reported values are the united root test statistics. The DF-GLS (Elliot et al., 1996) tests the null hypothesis of the existence of unit root. While the KPSS (Kwiatkowski et al., 1992) tests the null hypothesis of stationarity. The optimum lag length is selected on the basis of the AIC. *** denote significance at 1% level.

Table 3.4. BDS tests for stock returns

	m	ε(1)	ε(2)	ε(3)	ε(4)		m	ε(1)	ε(2)	ε(3)	ε(4)
Brazil	2	4.669	6.812	9.804	12.700	SA	2	7.414	9.005	10.453	11.537
	2	(0.000)	(0.000)	(0.000)	(0.000)		2	(0.000)	(0.000)	(0.000)	(0.000)
	3	7.749	10.280	13.489	16.672		3	11.509	13.579	15.571	17.061
	3	(0.000)	(0.000)	(0.000)	(0.000)		3	(0.000)	(0.000)	(0.000)	(0.000)
Chile	2	9.213	11.234	13.164	14.928	Turkey	2	8.213	10.025	11.832	13.370
	2	(0.000)	(0.000)	(0.000)	(0.000)		2	(0.000)	(0.000)	(0.000)	(0.000)
	3	11.666	13.771	15.697	17.383		3	11.506	13.746	15.518	16.700
	3	(0.000)	(0.000)	(0.000)	(0.000)		3	(0.000)	(0.000)	(0.000)	(0.000)
Colombia	2	14.850	17.357	18.947	20.186	UAE	2	7.520	8.796	10.292	12.520
	2	(0.000)	(0.000)	(0.000)	(0.000)		2	(0.000)	(0.000)	(0.000)	(0.000)
	3	18.752	20.804	22.684	24.253		3	6.237	8.776	10.373	12.922
	3	(0.000)	(0.000)	(0.000)	(0.000)		3	(0.000)	(0.000)	(0.000)	(0.000)
Mexico	2	7.980	10.450	12.444	13.301	China	2	8.491	9.563	10.887	11.306
	2	(0.000)	(0.000)	(0.000)	(0.000)		2	(0.000)	(0.000)	(0.000)	(0.000)
	3	11.330	14.542	16.758	17.441		3	12.882	14.168	15.349	14.948
	3	(0.000)	(0.000)	(0.000)	(0.000)		3	(0.000)	(0.000)	(0.000)	(0.000)
Peru	2	15.151	19.203	21.750	22.911	India	2	11.146	12.980	13.880	14.055
	2	(0.000)	(0.000)	(0.000)	(0.000)		2	(0.000)	(0.000)	(0.000)	(0.000)
	3	19.972	23.925	25.742	26.897		3	15.611	17.559	18.031	17.669
	3	(0.000)	(0.000)	(0.000)	(0.000)		3	(0.000)	(0.000)	(0.000)	(0.000)

Country	m	ε=0.5σ	ε=σ	ε=1.5σ	ε=2σ	Country	m	ε=0.5σ	ε=σ	ε=1.5σ	ε=2σ
CR	2	13.539	15.160	16.304	16.939	Indonesia	2	13.185	15.694	15.841	14.850
	2	(0.000)	(0.000)	(0.000)	(0.000)		2	(0.000)	(0.000)	(0.000)	(0.000)
	3	17.373	19.321	20.684	21.055		3	17.024	19.589	20.003	19.241
	3	(0.000)	(0.000)	(0.000)	(0.000)		3	(0.000)	(0.000)	(0.000)	(0.000)
Egypt	2	-0.234	5.229	8.828	9.814	Korea	2	8.005	9.875	11.574	12.806
	2	(0.815)	(0.000)	(0.000)	(0.000)		2	(0.000)	(0.000)	(0.000)	(0.000)
	3	2.197	8.608	11.914	12.563		3	11.205	13.772	15.925	17.430
	3	(0.028)	(0.000)	(0.000)	(0.000)		3	(0.000)	(0.000)	(0.000)	(0.000)
Greece	2	9.730	12.552	13.330	13.080	Malaysia	2	10.012	11.027	11.221	10.261
	2	(0.000)	(0.000)	(0.000)	(0.000)		2	(0.000)	(0.000)	(0.000)	(0.000)
	3	14.740	17.263	17.209	16.446		3	13.311	14.537	15.139	14.470
	3	(0.000)	(0.000)	(0.000)	(0.000)		3	(0.000)	(0.000)	(0.000)	(0.000)
Hungary	2	11.951	13.628	14.572	13.711	Pakistan	2	16.381	19.058	21.243	21.952
	2	(0.000)	(0.000)	(0.000)	(0.000)		2	(0.000)	(0.000)	(0.000)	(0.000)
	3	14.945	17.001	18.034	16.773		3	20.573	22.730	24.546	25.431
	3	(0.000)	(0.000)	(0.000)	(0.000)		3	(0.000)	(0.000)	(0.000)	(0.000)
Poland	2	7.717	9.027	10.741	11.703	Philippines	2	9.371	10.876	12.337	12.531
	2	(0.000)	(0.000)	(0.000)	(0.000)		2	(0.000)	(0.000)	(0.000)	(0.000)
	3	10.471	12.542	14.839	15.748		3	11.785	13.769	15.399	15.993
	3	(0.000)	(0.000)	(0.000)	(0.000)		3	(0.000)	(0.000)	(0.000)	(0.000)
Qatar	2	9.376	14.136	15.372	13.460	Taiwan	2	4.927	5.912	6.859	7.173
	2	(0.000)	(0.000)	(0.000)	(0.000)		2	(0.000)	(0.000)	(0.000)	(0.000)
	3	14.195	18.515	18.752	15.931		3	8.072	10.051	11.599	12.102
	3	(0.000)	(0.000)	(0.000)	(0.000)		3	(0.000)	(0.000)	(0.000)	(0.000)
Russia	2	10.556	11.803	12.338	12.139	Thailand	2	10.247	11.233	11.316	11.569
	2	(0.000)	(0.000)	(0.000)	(0.000)		2	(0.000)	(0.000)	(0.000)	(0.000)
	3	14.608	16.381	16.784	16.149		3	14.604	15.526	15.464	15.758
	3	(0.000)	(0.000)	(0.000)	(0.000)		3	(0.000)	(0.000)	(0.000)	(0.000)

Notes: The values represent the BDS test statistics and the *p*-values are reported within the parenthesis. The embedded dimensions are indicated by the parameter m and the epsilon values of close points are denoted by ε.

3.4.2. Linear model results

The author first unravels the linear association of oil price change and decomposed oil shocks with stock returns using a baseline linear regression. We follow the model specification expressed in Equation (4) and (5) and the results are reported in Table 3.5. The result of the univariate regression between oil price change and stock returns is presented in Panel A. The multivariate regression results between oil shocks and stock returns is exhibited in Panel B. The results from the univariate regression model shows that oil price change have a significant and positive impact on stock returns of all the markets with some marginal exception to India, Pakistan and Thailand where the relationship is positive, however statistically insignificant. Thus, the contemporaneous increase in stock returns is clearly evident in response to oil price change. We also plot the regression coefficients in Figure 3.7 in order to facilitate visual comparison. The value of coefficients ranges from 0.0083 (Pakistan) to 0.3283 (Russia). The positive relationship can be explained by the fact that the investors often relate the rising oil prices with a booming economy (Kollias et al., 2013). Similarly, Hamilton (2009a) also professes that prior to the GFC, higher business confidence in developing markets is reflected by the rising oil prices. Essentially, the concomitant impact on stock returns is driven by stronger business confidence in a flourishing economy. Undeniably, the EM have depicted phenomenal growth statistics in the recent years. For instance, the emerging economies have demonstrated strong economic growth trends. According to the World Bank estimates[34], the average growth rate of GDP in the EM in our sample set over the year 2013-17 is approximately 3.70%. Especially the Asian countries such as India (8.22%), China (8.20%) and Philippines (7.49) are exceptional.

Table 3. 5. Impact of oil price changes and shocks on stock returns

Panel A: Impact of oil prices changes				
	Constant	Δop_t	R squared	LL
Brazil [c]	0.0336	0.3068***	0.0920	-8937.735
	(0.948)	(20.159)		
Chile [b]	0.0421	0.1445***	0.0674	-6593.661
	(2.130)	(17.030)		
Colombia [a]	0.0512	0.2134***	0.0953	-7404.183
	(2.112)	(20.549)		
Mexico [a]	0.0265	0.2030***	0.0910	-7304.207
	(1.123)	(20.042)		
Peru [b]	0.0723	0.1946***	0.0907	-7141.884
	(3.191)	(20.005)		
CR [b]	0.0267	0.2100***	0.0853	-7582.563
	(1.058)	(19.346)		
Egypt [b]	0.1015	0.0343***	0.0018	-8186.454
	(3.456)	(2.714)		
Greece [b]	-0.0260	0.1798***	0.0424	-8458.060
	(-0.826)	(13.318)		
Hungary [b]	0.0311	0.2335***	0.0736	-8330.590
	(1.023)	(-17.852)		
Poland [c]	0.0335	0.2255***	0.0923	-7695.052
	(1.29)	(20.20)		
Qatar [a]	0.0385	0.0298***	0.0023	-7146.88
	(1.698)	(3.060)		
Russia [a]	0.0260	0.3283***	0.1010	-9000.75
	(0.721)	(21.233)		
SA [c]	0.0325	0.2504***	0.1905	-7734.392
	(1.238)	(22.209)		
Turkey [c]	0.0208	0.1856***	0.0336	-9066.476
	(0.568)	(11.813)		
UAE [a]	0.0416	0.0311***	0.0021	-7535.967
	(1.666)	(2.897)		
China [c]	0.0195	0.0585***	0.0074	-7525.512
	0.784	(5.467)		
India [c]	0.0482	0.1315	0.0358	-7553.696
	(1.920)	(12.20)		
Indonesia [c]	0.0549	0.0963***	0.0189	-7616.669
	(2.153)	(8.792)		
Korea [c]	0.0260	0.1398***	0.0361	-7782.582
	(0.979)	(12.248)		
Malaysia [b]	0.0194	0.0742***	0.0354	-5283.151
	(1.336)	(12.124)		
Pakistan [b]	0.0666	0.0083	0.0002	-6554.446
	(3.403)	(0.993)		

---

[34] The information is compiled and computed from the World Bank database. The complete data can be accessed at: https://data.worldbank.org/indicator/NY.GDP.MKTP.KD.ZG?year_high_desc=true, accessed 24/10/2018, 17:41 Hours, IST.

Philippines [b]	0.0435 (2.056)	0.0484*** (5.321)	0.0070		-6868.67
Taiwan [c]	0.0205 (0.989)	0.0741*** (8.340)	0.0171		-6780.388
Thailand [c]	0.0393 (1.900)	0.0894 (10.050)	0.0246		-6782.015

Panel B: Impact of oil shocks

	Constant	ds_t	ss_t	rs_t	R squared	LL
Brazil [c]	0.0359 (1.263)	0.8789*** (37.040)	-0.0415*** (-2.799)	-0.1570*** (-38.443)	0.4162	-8051.602
Chile [b]	0.0430 (2.586)	0.4197*** (30.260)	-0.0281*** (-3.243)	-0.0809*** (-33.873)	0.3409	-5897.194
Colombia [a]	0.535 (2.435)	0.4897*** (26.674)	0.0472*** (4.117)	-0.0789*** (-24.965)	0.2521	-7702.030
Mexico [a]	0.0275 (1.535)	0.5584*** (37.295)	-0.0338*** (-3.616)	-0.1214*** (-47.107)	0.4747	-6203.899
Peru [b]	0.0746 (3.702)	0.5289*** (31.429)	0.0123 (1.172)	-0.0693*** (-23.942)	0.2804	-6672.373
CR [b]	0.0295 (1.349)	0.6823*** (37.399)	-0.0246** (-2.157)	-0.0671*** (-21.366)	0.3169	-6996.857
Egypt [b]	0.1020 (3.486)	0.1492*** (6.109)	-0.0200 (-1.312)	-0.0118*** (-2.809)	0.0116	-8166.785
Greece [b]	-0.0243 (-0.832)	0.5376*** (22.068)	-0.0226 (-1.485)	-0.0801*** (-19.907)	0.1756	-8157.435
Hungary [b]	0.0339 (1.265)	0.7404*** (33.101)	-0.0293** (-2.100)	-0.0850*** (-22.085)	0.2837	-7814.512
Poland [c]	0.0362 (1.610)	0.6650*** (35.439)	-0.0083 (-0.7110)	-0.082*** (-25.447)	0.3220	-7109.623
Qatar [a]	0.0388 (1.720)	0.1145*** (6.079)	-0.0147 (-1.248)	-0.0141*** (-4.352)	0.0141	-7123.011
Russia [a]	0.0303 (0.3330)	0.9700*** (37.091)	0.0032 (0.1940)	-0.1018*** (-22.635)	0.3202	-8440.145
SA [c]	0.0353 (1.656)	0.7635*** (42.873)	-0.0232** (-2.084)	-0.0956*** (-31.175)	0.4125	-6900.022
Turkey [c]	0.0222 (0.652)	0.5735*** (20.180)	-0.0415** (-2.336)	-0.0946*** (-19.334)	0.1640	-8755.666
UAE [a]	0.0418 (1.686)	0.1369*** (6.611)	-0.0248* (-1.915)	-0.0174*** (-4.889)	0.0175	-7504.799
China [c]	0.0203 (0.822)	0.1842*** (8.937)	-0.0042 (-0.328)	-0.0184*** (-5.183)	0.0260	-7487.641
India [c]	0.0496 (2.110)	0.4312*** (21.971)	-0.0267** (-2.179)	-0.0529*** (-15.651)	0.1545	-7290.154
Indonesia [c]	0.0560 (2.292)	0.3690*** (18.088)	-0.0388*** (-3.047)	-0.0363*** (-10.336)	0.0996	-7444.525
Korea [c]	0.0276 (1.113)	0.4817*** (23.256)	-0.0344*** (-2.662)	-0.0524*** (-14.712)	0.1601	-7506.112
Malaysia [b]	0.0199 (1.468)	0.2240*** (19.728)	-0.0033 (-0.460)	-0.0253*** (-12.946)	0.1220	-5094.327
Pakistan [b]	0.0665 (3.407)	0.0389** (2.380)	-0.0086 (-0.843)	-0.0059** (-2.102)	0.0027	-6549.566
Philippines [b]	0.0441 (2.126)	0.2148*** (12.414)	-0.0316*** (-2.927)	-0.0185*** (-6.224)	0.0478	-6784.424
Taiwan [c]	0.0212 (1.066)	0.2765*** (16.655)	-0.0305*** (-2.937)	-0.0320*** (-11.191)	0.0930	-6618.934
Thailand [c]	0.0404 (2.053)	0.3306*** (20.107)	-0.0294*** (-2.865)	-0.0317*** (-11.210)	0.1184	-6579.204

Notes: The values represent the regression coefficients. The *t*-statistics is reported within the parenthesis. In Panel A, the results are obtained from the baseline regression specification as: $\Delta ret_{i,t} = \beta_{0,i} + \beta_{1,i}\Delta op_t + \mu_{i,t}$, where,

$\Delta ret_{i,t}$ represent the logarithmic returns of the stock prices. Δop_t denotes the oil price changes and $\mu_{i,t}$ is the random error term. For Panel B, the results are derived by the following regression specification: $\Delta ret_{i,t} = \beta_{0,i} + \beta_{1,i}ds_t + \beta_{2,i}ss_t + \beta_{3,i}rs_t + \mu_{i,t}$, the notations ds_t, ss_t and rs_t denotes the demand, supply and risk shocks respectively. LL denotes the values for loglikelihood. The 10%, 5% and 1% significance levels are denoted by *, ** and *** respectively. [a-] Exporters, [b-] Moderate importers and [c-] Importers

It must also be acknowledged that certain limitations are associated with using aggregate country-specific stock indexes. Mollick and Assefa (2013) argues that there is no reason to believe that oil price rise will impact the stock indexes uniformly since the index constituents are heterogeneous and sensitivity to the oil price fluctuations may be different. The oil price rise might invigorate the stocks of certain industrial sectors while it might dampen others. The varying degree of sensitivity of different indexes due to the role of index weight and composition is also highlighted by Aloui et al., (2012). In our sample set, the regression coefficient of Russia (*see* Table 3.6, Panel A) is the maximum despite of low GDP growth rate of 0.19% over 2013-17. Given the theoretical guidelines of Kollias et al., (2013) and Hamilton (2009a), this relationship is somewhat paradoxical. It must be noted that Russia is a major oil and gas exporter and the MICEX index constitutes stocks from energy sector that aggregates about 42.09%, which is also highest among all the other indexes.[35] Thus, the increasing oil prices is expected to increase the earnings of the energy sectors and hence the oil-price relationship is significant and positive.

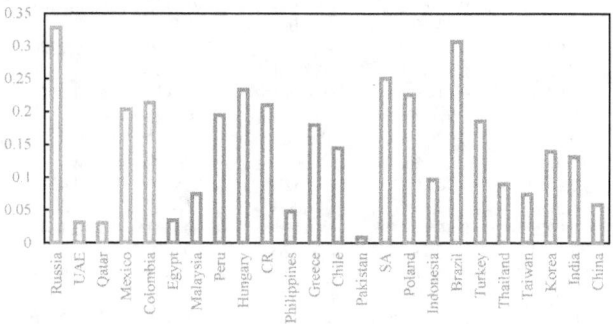

Figure 3.7. Coefficient plot of oil price changes on stock returns
Notes: The columns with Green, Blue and Red bounds represents the coefficients for the exporters, moderate importers and importers respectively.

Notwithstanding, with the economic growth hypothesis and index weights, we observe relatively small coefficient value of UAE and Qatar (*see* Table 3.6, Panel A and Figure 3.7). All must recognize the fact that both UAE and Qatar are OPEC member countries. The prime objective of OPEC is the unification and co-ordination of petroleum policies for providing efficient, economic and uninterrupted supplies to the oil-importing countries at secure, stable and fair prices. On account of their price regulation authority the equity investors in those countries may not panic much over the oil price shocks. The investor sentiments may also play a crucial role in this case, which is readily recognized in the oil-stock behavior literature (*see*

---

[35] The energy sector firms are likely to benefit with increasing oil prices. The major energy sector firms in MICEX index are LUKOIL Holding, GAZPROM, TATNEFT, NOVATEK GDR, ROSNEFT etc. The composition details of the MICEX index are available at: https://www.moex.com/a1177, accessed 25/10/2018, 00:03 Hours, IST.

Chen et al., (2017)). Besides, UAE and Qatar are also undergoing the phase of economic reconstruction where a paradigm shift of these economies is observed. These economies are traditionally oil-dependent since oil and gas are rich natural sources available to these countries in abundance. However, these countries have gradually diversified their economies to other segments, which is inevitable in the due course with the emergence of alternative energy sources. Both UAE and Qatar have exhibited remarkable commitment in the process of sectoral diversification. In 1975, the contribution of oil towards the national GDP of UAE was 60%, which has now been curbed down to 30% by 2017. The share of oil is replaced by real estate, retail, financial and business services.[36] Similarly, for Qatar the non-hydrocarbon contribution to national GDP has increased as much as 60% by 2017.[37]

Besides it is also important to understand the role of government intervention though the transfer payments in developing economies. The rising oil prices worries the government for both economic and political reasons. Thus, in order to insulate the consumers from the oil price shocks government allows for transfer payments in the form of subsidies.[38] For example, due to recent oil price surges the fuel subsidy by Indian government has ballooned up by ₹ 530 billion by the fiscal year ending at March 2019[39]. Aloui et al., (2012) also emphasizes upon the role of transfer payments to understand the oil-stock relationship. Thus, the notion related to the positive (negative) impact of oil price rise on oil-exporting (importing) countries on stock returns is conditioned upon several crucial factors as we discuss above (besides there could be many others). Considering the diverse economic facets that disrupt the natural oil-stock relationship, it is difficult to explain the relationship using a single theoretical framework in isolation.

Next, we move on to Panel B, the results are obtained using the disentangled oil price shocks as specified in Equation 5. We find that the demand shock is positively associated with the stock returns for all the cases consistent with Ready (2018). As we have discussed earlier, positive relationship is expected between demand shock and stock returns since oil demand is associated with booming economy. As we can follow from the coefficient plot in Figure 3.8 (a), Russia, Brazil, SA are at the top. These three countries are also the part of fast-growing subset of emerging economies, namely the BRICS. On the other hand, the coefficient of Pakistan is at the bottom, however positive, signifying a low sensitivity of stock returns to demand-specific shocks. The relationship of stock returns and supply shock is negative for all the countries with exception to Colombia, Peru and Russia. It must be mentioned that Colombia and Russia are oil exporters, the oil exporting countries are likely to inherit a natural hedge to oil shocks. Supply shocks are essentially the rise in oil prices due to oil supply side cost

---

[36] For the complete report kindly refer article "*Is the UAE moving away from oil?*" (2018). Available at: https://www.financialexpress.com/opinion/is-the-uae-moving-away-from-oil/1315453/, accessed 25/10/2018, 14:15 Hours, IST.
[37] For the complete report kindly refer article "*Qatar lauded for diversifying economy away from oil, gas*" (2017). Available at: https://www.gulf-times.com/story/563719/Qatar-lauded-for-diversifying-economy-away-from-oi, accessed 25/10/2018, 14:25 Hours, IST.
[38] For the complete report kindly refer article "*Oil Price Subsidies—How Are Developing Countries Adjusting to $100 Oil?*" (2013), Available at: http://blogs.worldbank.org/energy/oil-price-subsidies-how-are-developing-countries-adjusting-100-oil, accessed 26/10/2018, 14:12 Hours, IST and also see "*Energy subsidies in developing countries: Treating the disease while symptoms abate*" (2015), Available at: https://voxeu.org/article/energy-subsidies-developing-countries, accessed 26/10/2018, 14:16 Hours, IST.
[39] The full report is available at: https://energy.economictimes.indiatimes.com/news/oil-and-gas/high-oil-price-india-staring-at-fuel-subsidy-burden-up-to-rs-53000-crore/64268245, accessed 26/10/2018, 14:36 Hours, IST.

impulse. Thus, the exporters might sell less units of oil at a high price to recover its cost and maintain the desired profit margin. In the case of Peru, though the coefficient is statistically insignificant, the positive value owes some implications. Peru has initiated diversification of energy use and gradually transforming itself from moderate importer to exporter of Liquified Natural Gas (LNG) since 2004-05.[40]

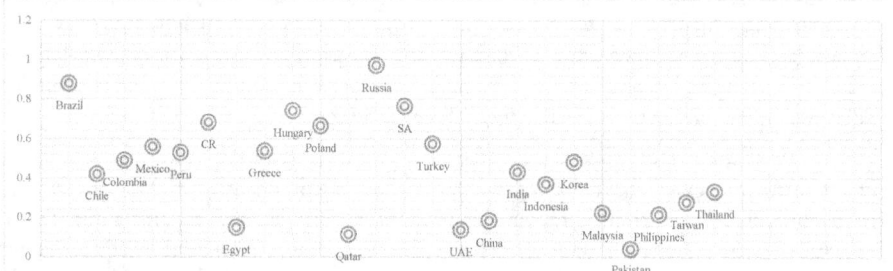

(a) Demand shock

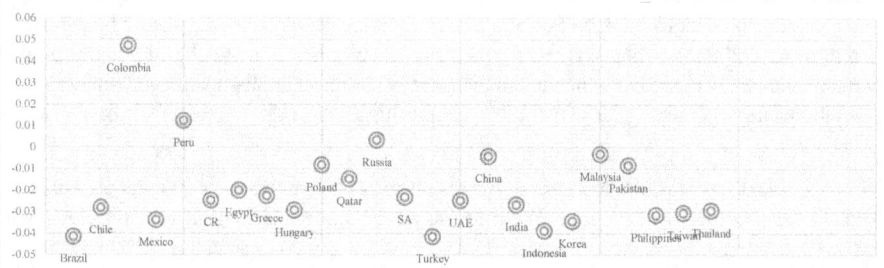

(b) Supply shock

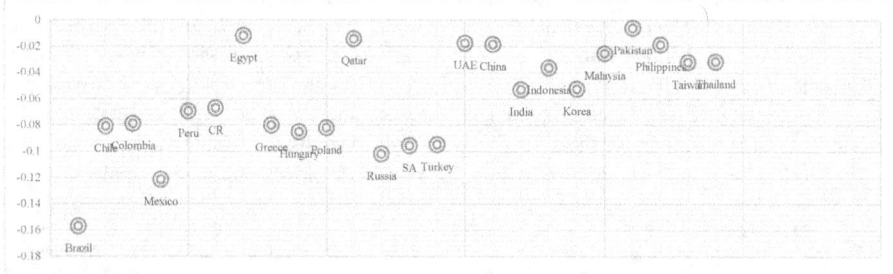

(c) Risk shock

Figure 3.8. Coefficient plot of demand, supply and risk shocks

---

[40] The central bank of Peru is likely to invest 12% of national budget by 2018-19. The full report is available at: http://www.rree.gob.pe/Documents/Guia_de_inversiones_hidrocarburos_2018.pdf, accessed 26/10/2018, 14:36 Hours, IST.

The risk shocks are basically innovations in the VIX. Since, the VIX is also known as the fear gauge of investors (Whaley, 2000), a negative relationship is expected with the stock returns. We can easily infer from Table 3.6, Panel B and Figure 3.8 (c) that the relationship is negative and significant for all the markets. The minimum negative value is observed for Pakistan implying the least negative impact of risk-based shocks. Whereas the highest negative value is observed for Brazil. Further, we compare the R square of model specification expressed in Equation 4 and 5. The comparison of the R square values is presented in Figure 3.9. The explanatory power of the model with disentangled oil price shocks is clearly improved as compared to the model that simply considers the oil price changes. The improvement in the R square for some of the countries such as Egypt, Qatar, UAE, China and Pakistan are marginally improved or nearly unchanged. These countries also show lower sensitivity to oil price changes (*see* Table 3.6, Panel A and Figure 3.7). The explanatory power for some countries has improved such as for Greece, Russia, Turkey, India, Indonesia, Korea, Malaysia, Philippines, Taiwan and Thailand, however inconsequentially. Uddin et al., (2018) in this respect argues that lower value of R square may be an outcome of violation of linearity assumption as a result of biased model specification. Therefore, we resort to nonlinear model in the next segment of the .

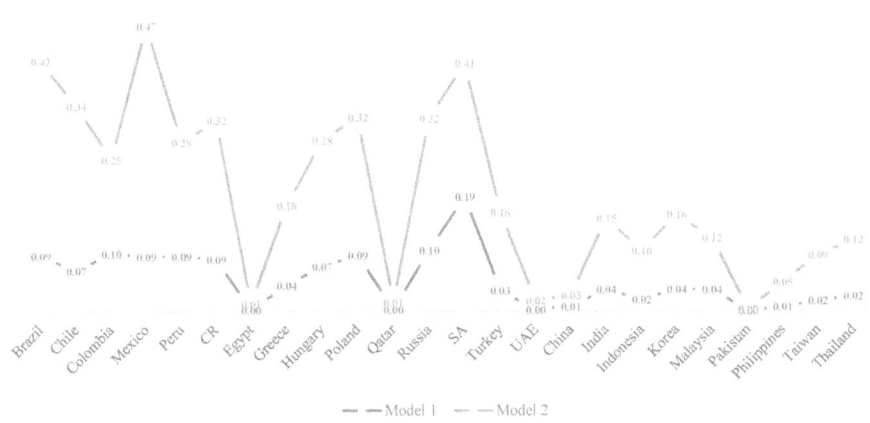

Figure 3.9. Comparison of the R square
Notes: The Model 1 and 2 is referred to the R square obtained for the model specifications mentioned in Equation 4 and 5 respectively.

3.4.3. Markov regime switching model results

The estimation results for the multi-factor and two-state MRS model is reported in Table 3.7. The estimated coefficients are reported in Panel A, whereas the information regarding transition probabilities and expected durations are reported in Panel B. In the estimation process we use two different distribution assumption of error terms, they are student's t distribution (t) and Normal distribution (N). The estimation using the t distribution assumption is relatively stable over the N distribution assumption. The causal reason being in the tranquil period a single outlier of large innovation may lead to a switch over to high volatility regime when the residuals are normally distributed (Basher et al., 2016). Thus, Basher et al., (2016) and Uddin et al., (2018) use both the assumptions separately to show the robustness checks. We also follow both the assumptions following previous studies. However, we encounter some computational issues in the estimation process similar to Basher et al., (2016).[41] While estimating the MRS model using the t distribution specification we find 13 out of 24 time-series revert the entries as NA (not available) for standard errors.[42] Basher et al., (2016) clearly states that when the properties of the data is not completely captured by the distribution assumption such problems may occur in the numerically intensive optimization computations.[43] Thus, we report the results with t distribution assumption where no error is occurred. Besides, we also compare the RCM before doing so, since lower value of RCM signifies better classification of regimes. The underlying distribution assumption is indicated as superscript on the RCM values in Panel B.

Table 3.6. The impact of oil price shocks on stock returns- Markov regime switching models

Panel A: Estimated coefficients							
Markets	State	Constant	ds_t	ss_t	rs_t	Sigma	LL
Brazil [c]	S_1	0.0594	0.8844***	-0.0494***	-0.160***	1.321***	-7600.930
		(2.475)	(35.923)	(-3.406)	(-39.472)	(64.673)	
	S_2	-0.0753	0.883***	-0.030	-0.1482***	3.154***	
		(-0.622)	(13.095)	(-0.650)	(-9.543)	(29.709)	
Chile [b]	S_1	0.100	0.367***	-0.025***	-0.065***	0.703***	-5439.437
		(6.072)	(21.678)	(-2.774)	(-27.620)	(38.977)	
	S_2	-0.091	0.387***	-0.032	-0.106***	1.179***	
		(-1.994)	(12.070)	(-1.620)	(-15.486)	(23.207)	
Colombia [a]	S_1	-0.065	0.463***	0.072	-0.130***	2.690***	-6385.289
		(-0.551)	(7.412)	(1.420)	(-8.844)	(22.143)	
	S_2	0.085	0.465***	0.048***	-0.065***	0.960***	
		(4.738)	(22.835)	(4.840)	(-23.377)	(44.509)	
Mexico [a]	S_1	0.041	0.464***	-0.036***	-0.115***	0.856***	-5801.461
		(2.630)	(25.577)	(-3.832)	(-40.904)	(52.508)	
	S_2	-0.046	0.693***	-0.004	-0.129***	2.132***	
		(-0.468)	(13.119)	(-0.111)	(-11.391)	(20.697)	
Peru [b]	S_1	0.092	0.770***	0.028	-0.102***	1.362***	-5741.642
		(1.733)	(15.739)	(1.035)	(-14.236)	(21.135)	
	S_2	0.067	0.302***	0.011	-0.044***	0.645***	
		(4.468)	(18.137)	(1.267)	(-18.630)	(38.071)	
CR [b]	S_1	0.042	0.663***	-0.074***	-0.115***	0.991***	-6452.741
		(1.323)	(22.200)	(-3.579)	(-23.032)	(33.853)	
	S_2	0.045	0.194***	-0.058***	-0.028***	0.756***	
		(2.077)	(8.801)	(-4.218)	(-9.230)	(35.971)	
Egypt [b]	S_1	0.222	0.071***	-0.023**	-0.002	0.927**	-7296.939
		(11.255)	(3.699)	(-1.962)	(-0.753)	(27.026)	
	S_2	-0.358	0.271***	0.002	-0.038**	3.563**	
		(-2.640)	(3.174)	(0.035)	(-2.167)	(26.443)	
Greece [b]	S_1	-0.137	0.620***	0.000	-0.104***	2.416***	-7616.631
		(-2.384)	(14.268)	(0.015)	(-13.221)	(42.911)	
	S_2	0.109	0.286***	-0.054***	-0.038***	1.017***	
		(4.304)	(9.776)	(-3.978)	(-9.171)	(37.220)	
Hungary [b]	S_1	-0.107	0.982***	0.032	-0.103***	2.469	-7336.162

---

[41] The author has also used the same software package as used by Basher et al., (2016) for performing the MRS regression i.e. fMarkovswitching package in R environment.
[42] In addition, the estimation process that fails to return the standards errors also does a poor job in regime classification which is indicated by the higher RCM values.
[43] See footnote 12 of Basher et al., (2016).

Country							
		(-1.429)	(19.507)	(0.952)	(-9.926)	(34.894)	
	S_2	0.099	0.404***	-0.048***	-0.057***	1.164	
		(4.292)	(14.260)	(-3.692)	(-15.007)	(58.440)	
Poland [c]	S_1	0.027	0.999***	0.041	-0.108***	1.308***	-6660.142
		(0.639)	(22.026)	(1.608)	(-16.372)	(25.562)	
	S_2	0.071	0.334***	-0.049***	-0.050***	0.911***	
		(3.302)	(12.483)	(-3.994)	(-13.050)	(35.022)	
Qatar [a]	S_1	0.037	0.186***	-0.026	-0.028***	2.283***	-5725.491
		(0.615)	(4.251)	(-0.949)	(-3.387)	(34.739)	
	S_2	0.044	0.033***	-0.003	-0.002*	0.377***	
		(4.461)	(3.434)	(-0.472)	(-1.663)	(15.330)	
Russia [a]	S_1	-0.128	1.084***	0.004	-0.104***	3.611	-7658.275
		(-0.986)	(14.739)	(0.078)	(-5.684)	(31.044)	
	S_2	0.075	0.849***	0.007	-0.095***	1.237	
		(3.225)	(32.122)	(0.449)	(-26.882)	(54.419)	
SA [c]	S_1	-0.050	0.751***	0.038	-0.093***	1.601***	-6510.445
		(-0.778)	(15.163)	(1.503)	(-11.664)	(17.521)	
	S_2	0.064	0.806***	-0.085***	-0.101***	0.937***	
		(-1.277)	(15.837)	(1.532)	(-7.091)	(22.154)	
Turkey [c]	S_1	0.082	0.576***	-0.077***	-0.084***	1.543***	-8305.848
		(2.768)	(15.913)	(-4.057)	(-17.590)	(51.722)	
	S_2	-0.188	0.529***	0.043	-0.138***	3.684***	
		(-1.348)	(6.273)	(0.775)	(-7.101)	(28.105)	
UAE [a]	S_1	0.027	0.242***	-0.045	-0.031***	2.222***	-5453.153
		(0.531)	(6.009)	(-1.802)	(-4.409)	(48.446)	
	S_2	0.057	0.004	0.003	-0.002***	0.166***	
		(11.445)	(1.104)	(1.070)	(-2.356)	(14.744)	
China [c]	S_1	-0.058	0.185***	-0.004	-0.037***	2.620***	-6860.171
		(-0.660)	(3.574)	(-0.111)	(-3.397)	(33.455)	
	S_2	0.053	0.160***	-0.002	-0.008***	0.994***	
		(2.669)	(7.463)	(-0.196)	(-2.381)	(47.832)	
India [c]	S_1	-0.082	0.559***	-0.005	-0.068***	2.385***	-6684.890
		(-1.046)	(12.113)	(-0.156)	(-6.437)	(27.296)	
	S_2	0.103	0.264***	-0.027***	-0.038***	0.967***	
		(4.955)	(11.788)	(-2.342)	(-12.173)	(36.446)	
Indonesia [c]	S_1	-0.127	0.451***	-0.021	-0.032***	1.970***	-6657.973
		(-1.497)	(7.915)	(-0.614)	(-2.999)	(16.954)	
	S_2	0.137	0.232***	-0.032***	-0.028***	0.812***	
		(7.589)	(11.161)	(-2.863)	(-9.912)	(35.833)	
Korea [c]	S_1	-0.038	0.517***	-0.031	-0.044***	1.831***	-6697.848
		(-0.524)	(10.692)	(-1.099)	(-4.203)	(19.468)	
	S_2	0.101	0.367***	-0.040***	-0.044***	0.863***	
		(5.509)	(16.346)	(-3.345)	(-15.067)	(37.426)	
Malaysia [b]	S_1	0.016	0.274***	-0.010	-0.028***	0.864***	-4556.643
		(0.615)	(13.271)	(-0.817)	(-7.727)	(23.811)	
	S_2	0.037	0.127***	0.006	-0.015***	0.467***	
		(3.157)	(7.388)	(0.797)	(-6.167)	(28.256)	
Pakistan [b]	S_1	0.153	0.015	-0.008	-0.005***	0.646***	-5810.538
		(10.537)	(1.326)	(-1.016)	(-2.269)	(36.780)	
	S_2	-0.289	0.103	-0.009	-0.008	2.153***	
		(-3.375)	(1.661)	(-0.276)	(-0.670)	(19.139)	
Philippines [b]	S_1	0.042	0.257***	-0.066***	-0.010	1.465***	-6340.988
		(0.850)	(6.860)	(-2.778)	(-1.468)	(19.329)	
	S_2	0.073	0.119***	0.004	-0.017***	0.802***	
		(3.734)	(5.218)	(0.359)	(-5.445)	(31.707)	
Taiwan [c]	S_1	-0.132	0.323***	-0.015	-0.031***	1.942***	-6133.727
		(-2.149)	(9.074)	(-0.662)	(-4.131)	(38.427)	
	S_2	0.084	0.211***	-0.036***	-0.028***	0.850***	
		(4.968)	(10.869)	(-3.349)	(-10.034)	(55.175)	
Thailand [c]	S_1	-0.005	0.360***	-0.007	-0.028***	1.269***	-5948.021

	(-0.145)	(13.470)	(-0.431)	(-5.756)	(25.109)
S_2	0.098	0.232***	-0.040***	-0.027***	0.628***
	(5.875)	(10.884)	(-2.937)	(-10.312)	(27.275)

Panel B: Transition probabilities and expected durations

	P_{11}	P_{12}	P_{21}	P_{22}	DU_1	DU_2	RCM
Brazil [c]	0.989	0.011	0.050	0.950	90.752	20.065	30.180^N
Chile [b]	0.987	0.013	0.029	0.971	77.688	34.695	30.280^N
Colombia [a]	0.9047	0.0953	0.0177	0.9823	10.498	56.427	39.726^t
Mexico [a]	0.978	0.022	0.136	0.864	45.147	7.368	57.805^N
Peru [b]	0.963	0.037	0.015	0.985	27.195	64.864	25.369^t
CR [b]	0.984	0.016	0.084	0.916	63.104	11.942	29.700^t
Egypt [b]	0.860	0.140	0.512	0.488	7.134	1.952	66.340^N
Greece [b]	0.970	0.030	0.024	0.976	33.181	41.141	21.471^N
Hungary [b]	0.967	0.033	0.014	0.986	29.955	73.489	23.866^N
Poland [c]	0.986	0.014	0.009	0.991	69.646	116.874	22.101^t
Qatar [a]	0.564	0.436	0.257	0.743	2.293	3.889	46.456^N
Russia [a]	0.934	0.066	0.017	0.983	15.212	58.160	27.374^N
SA [c]	0.977	0.023	0.009	0.991	43.792	117.357	28.290^t
Turkey [c]	0.985	0.015	0.061	0.939	65.538	16.402	35.498^N
UAE [a]	0.535	0.465	0.447	0.553	2.149	2.236	26.619^N
China [c]	0.938	0.062	0.020	0.980	16.093	49.296	29.843^N
India [c]	0.956	0.044	0.015	0.985	22.643	64.647	24.691^N
Indonesia [c]	0.947	0.053	0.017	0.983	18.840	59.288	35.138^t
Korea [c]	0.986	0.014	0.005	0.995	72.401	205.891	18.150^t
Malaysia [b]	0.991	0.009	0.006	0.994	106.901	159.019	19.844^t
Pakistan [b]	0.983	0.017	0.069	0.931	58.085	14.506	33.485^t
Philippines [b]	0.967	0.033	0.018	0.982	30.503	54.143	34.179^t
Taiwan [c]	0.966	0.034	0.013	0.987	29.208	74.712	23.032^N
Thailand [c]	0.983	0.017	0.016	0.984	58.056	64.035	22.510^t

Notes: The table reports the results of Markov regime switching model of the following functional form: $\Delta ret_{i,t} = \beta_{0,i,\, r_t} + \beta_{1,i,\, r_t} ds_t + \beta_{2,i,\, r_t} ss_t + \beta_{3,i,\, r_t} rs_t + \mu_{i,t}$, the notations $\Delta ret_{i,t}$ represent the logarithmic returns of the stock prices and ds_t, ss_t and rs_t denotes the demand, supply and risk shocks respectively. The r_t is a discrete regime variable and the regime dependent intercept is noted as $\beta_{0,i,\, r_t}$. The slope coefficients are represented as $\beta_{1,i,\, r_t} ds_t \ldots \ldots \beta_{3,i,\, r_t} rs_t$. The $\mu_{i,t}$ is the random error term. LL denotes the values for loglikelihood. The superscript t and N denote the student's t and Normal distribution assumption of the error terms respectively. DU is the expected duration in a regime. The 10%, 5% and 1% significance levels are denoted by *, ** and *** respectively.
[a]- Exporters, [b]- Moderate importers and [c]- Importers

The volatility conditions are determined by the values of sigma. State 2 is the high volatility condition for the markets such as of Brazil, Chile, Mexico, Egypt, Turkey and Pakistan. State 1 is high volatile for rest of the markets. As we find in the linear specification, demand shock is positively associated with stock returns. On the other hand, supply and risk related shocks is negatively related. Regarding the demand shocks, we do not observe much regime-dependent change in the value of coefficients. Nonetheless, we observe an interesting regime-dependent finding in respect of the supply shocks. We find the supply shocks to be significant for low volatility state and significant otherwise for 17 out of 24 markets in the sample, the exceptions are CR, Peru, Philippines, Qatar, Russia, China and Malaysia. This shows that negative impact of oil supply shocks to stocks is overwhelming when markets are relatively stable. Antithetically, when markets are jittery oil supply shocks show insignificant predictability of stock returns. The financial and behavioral factors could be more crucial determinants for predicting the stock returns behavior when the market states are turbulent. For example, during the events of financial crises the consumers curb down (or postpone) their propensity to consume and thus there will be overall less demand for any commodity and the firms thus, will tend to produce less to match the revised level of demand at existing prices (firms may not increase the prices per unit since that may lead to further fall in demand). Thus, when markets are already turbulent coupled up with diminishing demand (causing limited production by firms) the oil price rise due to supply shocks is expected to have marginal spillover on the stock prices. Moreover, there could also be a possibility that the impact of financial and behavioral factors is strong enough to overshadow the influence of supply shocks. Regime-independent behavior is observed for risk shocks suggesting that the innovations in VIX has negative implications for all the markets. We further find that the loglikelihood value (LL) is improved for the MRS model as compared to LL reported in Table 3.6, the LL statistic is maximized.[44] Hence, the MRS model performance is found superior to linear models similar to Uddin et al., (2018).

Panel B provides certain relevant inferences on regime transition. The column on the extreme right represents the measure concerning the model accuracy i.e. RCM. The lower value of RCM is desirable since it denotes better classification of regime. We find that the values range from 18.150 for Korea to 66.340 for Egypt. Nevertheless, the RCM statistic take values from 0 to 100, thus, overall the MRS model fits well to the series under consideration.[45] Figure 3.10 (a) plots the index of Korea and the corresponding filtered probabilities for high and low volatility regimes are presented in Figure 3.10 (b) and (c) respectively.[46] Dense and peaked iceberg-like structure is observed particularly around the period 2008-09 in Figure 3.10 (b) signifying high volatility during GFC. The Korean market is however stable since 2012. Figure 3.10 (c) is residual filtered probabilities of Figure 3.10 (b) i.e. the peaked structures depict low volatility regime. The DU stands for the expected duration of halt in one regime. The general behavior of the markets shows higher halting duration in low volatility state than otherwise. This result is consistent with the conventional wisdom that the tranquil spells in the markets are more consistent than undesirable turbulent phases (Basher et al., 2018). Lastly, we also find large constant regime probabilities of P_{11} and P_{22}, which depict high persistence of each regime for all the markets similar to Basher et al., (2016) and Uddin et al., (2018).

---

[44] Readers must note that all the values of LL are negative and the MRS model maximizes (or improves) the LL statistic. Thus, for example, -10 is better than -20 i.e. lower negative values are better. The readers should not get confused by the statement in the main text.
[45] Besides, we also test the appropriateness of MRS by conducting the BDS test on the residuals of the MRS model following Uddin et al., (2018). We find that the series residuals are close approximates of *iid*. We do not report the result of the repeated test for brevity.
[46] The does not plot all the indexes and corresponding filtered probabilities for saving space.

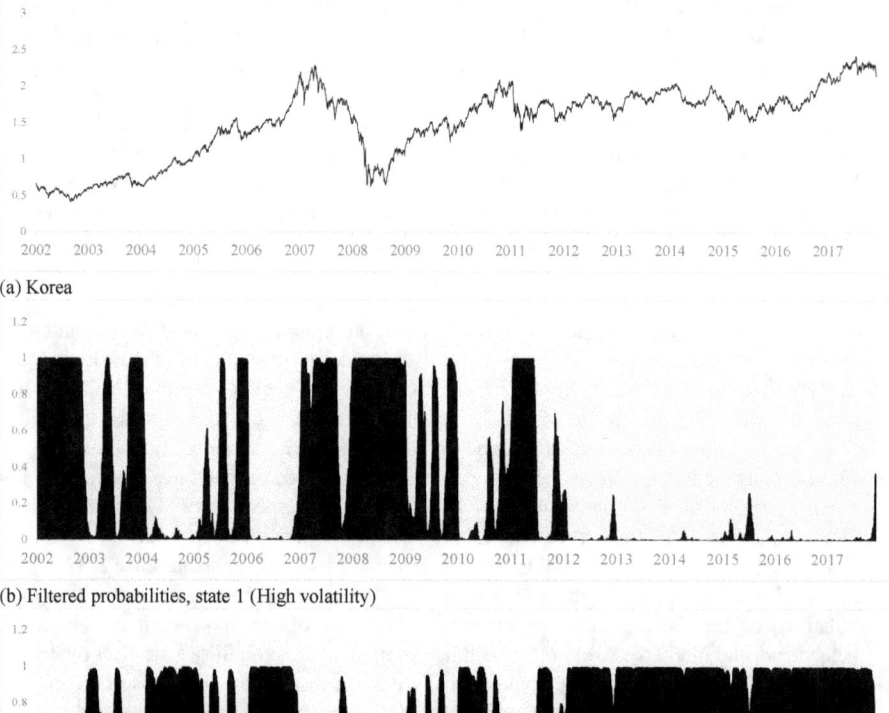

(a) Korea

(b) Filtered probabilities, state 1 (High volatility)

(c) Filtered probabilities, state 2 (Low volatility)

Figure 3.10. Stock price index and filtered probabilities plot of Korea

3.4.4. Quantile regression model results

The author further uses QR model with breaks to understand the behavior of stock returns in response to oil shocks for the full period and onset the GFC at different market returns conditions. The QR analysis complements the results of the linear and MRS model. The author reports seven quantiles between 0.05 to 0.95. The quantiles 0.05-0.25 represents the bearish market state, whereas quantiles 0.75-0.95 denotes the bullish market states. Quantile 0.50 stands for the normal market state. The β denotes the marginal effect of oil price shocks for the full period while ignoring the GFC break. Whereas the δ signifies the dependence structure onset the GFC of 2008. Our broad findings of linear and MRS model is somewhat consistent with QR results, however, additional insights are documented. Regarding the demand shocks, we find statistically significant and positive association, nonetheless, the structure and degree of dependence varies considerably over the quantiles. For the Brazilian stock market, the dependence intensifies monotonically from lower to higher quantiles for the full sample period. However, a reverse behavior is observed for the period onset GFC i.e. the degree of dependence decays gradually towards the upper tail. The demand shock β for all other markets (with exception to Qatar and Malaysia) are usually is higher at lower tail ($Q_{0.05}$, bearish) than the upper tail ($Q_{0.95}$, bullish). The tail behavior of δ is somewhat opposite to the β behavior in the case of all other markets with Philippines, Malaysia, China and UAE. The behavior of the intermediate quantiles is heterogeneous across all the markets.

Similarly, the supply shock β and δ is mostly negative and significant across all quantiles. However, some positive and significant β and δ coefficients are observed for Russia, UAE, Mexico and Colombia. According to the theoretical postulates the relationship is expected to be negative, but we must consider that these countries are exporters. As we have discussed earlier, the exporters inherit a natural hedge against the oil shocks. The rising oil production costs can be mitigated by quoting higher selling price to maintain profit margin while offsetting the impact lower quantity demanded due to price rise. Furthermore, we also find that there is no such strong common behavior across all the markets besides the sign of the coefficients also switches from negative to positive though it is statistically insignificant. However, evidences of comparatively strong lower tail dependencies occur frequently. The risk shocks are negative and significant for almost all the markets with some exceptions. For instance, Brazil, Chile and Colombia depict some positive coefficients for the risk shock δ, there could be a plausible underlying economic reasoning rather than simply a statistical stylized fact that is the EM are also viewed as suitable avenues for international portfolio diversification (Grubel, 1968; Levy and Sarnat, 1970). Thus, when the US markets are volatile as depicted by the VIX, the investors may show a transitory behavior to the EM. Thus, positive co-movements might occur between risk shocks and EM stock markets. Nevertheless, in our sample set, the negative coefficients for both β and δ dominates over the positive counterparts and the degree of dependence is usually stronger at the lower tails.

Table 3.7. The estimation results of the bootstrapped quantile regression

Market		Quantiles						
		$Q_{0.05}$	$Q_{0.10}$	$Q_{0.25}$	$Q_{0.50}$	$Q_{0.75}$	$Q_{0.90}$	$Q_{0.95}$
Brazil [c]	β_{ds}	0.489***	0.615***	0.696***	0.712***	0.691***	0.685***	0.872***
	δ_{ds}	0.461***	0.338***	0.293***	0.279***	0.264***	0.280*	0.205
	β_{ss}	-0.150*	-0.122**	-0.126***	-0.091***	-0.0529**	-0.0920**	-0.0416
	δ_{ss}	0.131	0.095	-0.091**	-0.091***	0.0536	-0.120*	0.0473
	β_{rs}	-0.224***	-0.205***	-0.200***	-0.203***	-0.201***	-0.183***	-0.184***
	δ_{rs}	0.068*	0.052**	0.065***	0.061***	0.060***	0.046**	0.034
	γ	0.421***	0.269*	-0.010	-0.147***	-0.279***	-0.483***	-0.403**
	α	-2.932***	-2.092***	-0.887***	0.137***	1.179***	2.289***	3.021***
Chile [b]	β_{ds}	0.273***	0.238***	0.239***	0.247***	0.284***	0.222***	0.219***
	δ_{ds}	0.229**	0.258***	0.197***	0.197***	0.166***	0.236***	0.271***
	β_{ss}	-0.0415	-0.073***	-0.052***	-0.061***	-0.046***	-0.0153	-0.0617*
	δ_{ss}	0.00696	0.0186	0.013	0.0355	0.0259	0.0107	0.0674
	β_{rs}	-0.100***	-0.095***	-0.087***	-0.079***	-0.078***	-0.078***	-0.085***
	δ_{rs}	0.014	0.0116	0.0123	0.00737	0.00793*	0.011	0.0111
	γ	0.111	0.122**	0.000616	-0.0650**	-0.185***	-0.137***	-0.0368
	α	-1.588***	-1.176***	-0.515***	0.0945***	0.750***	1.281***	1.640***
Colombia [a]	β_{ds}	0.460***	0.454***	0.328***	0.176***	0.213***	0.241***	0.282***
	δ_{ds}	0.0702	0.123	0.209***	0.351***	0.343***	0.365***	0.294***
	β_{ss}	0.0753	-0.034	0.040*	0.0253	0.000548	0.0155	0.0188
	δ_{ss}	0.0229	0.103*	0.0196	0.030	0.053**	0.0428	0.036
	β_{rs}	-0.141***	-0.105***	-0.080***	-0.056***	-0.037***	-0.058***	-0.070***

Mexico [a]	δ_{rs}	0.0594**	0.023	0.010	-0.0113	-0.032***	-0.0167	0.00131
	γ	0.671***	0.358***	0.0447	-0.136***	-0.368***	-0.549***	-0.730***
	α	-2.465***	-1.584***	-0.620***	0.144***	0.975***	1.861***	2.500***
	β_{ds}	0.435***	0.486***	0.427***	0.336***	0.309***	0.364***	0.313***
	δ_{ds}	0.122	0.0613	0.183***	0.279***	0.303***	0.316***	0.352***
	β_{ss}	-0.083***	-0.0449*	-0.0213	-0.043***	-0.072***	-0.076***	-0.0716
	δ_{ss}	0.0664	0.0109	-0.0266	0.0161	0.0579***	0.0446	0.0338
	β_{rs}	-0.153***	-0.137***	-0.141***	-0.139***	-0.138***	-0.149***	-0.143***
	δ_{rs}	0.0280*	0.0177*	0.0228***	0.0277***	0.0261***	0.0442***	0.0350**
	γ	0.0851	0.0173	-0.0646*	-0.0803**	-0.102***	-0.0729	0.00278
	α	-1.711***	-1.225***	-0.512***	0.105***	0.703***	1.298***	1.723***
Peru [b]	β_{ds}	0.490***	0.526***	0.337***	0.267***	0.270***	0.275***	0.271*
	δ_{ds}	0.0414	0.00869	0.157***	0.241***	0.305***	0.417***	0.421**
	β_{ss}	0.0413	0.00261	0.00696	0.00655	0.0331	0.00746	0.042
	δ_{ss}	-0.0283	0.0167	0.00832	-0.0122	-0.0581**	-0.0347	-0.0345
	β_{rs}	-0.077***	-0.057***	-0.047***	-0.042***	-0.053***	-0.060***	-0.068***
	δ_{rs}	-0.00727	-0.0262**	-0.0215**	-0.023***	-0.0118	-0.00711	-0.00288
	γ	-0.141	-0.0923	-0.0753	-0.134***	-0.145**	-0.275***	-0.440***
	α	-1.677***	-1.120***	-0.446***	0.153***	0.748***	1.534***	2.217***
CR [b]	β_{ds}	0.654***	0.596***	0.489***	0.416***	0.378***	0.360***	0.439***
	δ_{ds}	0.0632	0.0645	0.179***	0.226***	0.304***	0.388***	0.367***
	β_{ss}	-0.00747	-0.0546	-0.0151	-0.044***	-0.0186	-0.017	0.00732
	δ_{ss}	0.00728	0.0174	-0.055*	-0.0268	-0.0592*	-0.0438	-0.0542
	β_{rs}	-0.070***	-0.061***	-0.052***	-0.042***	-0.033***	-0.039***	-0.037***
	δ_{rs}	-0.0299**	-0.0266*	-0.0228**	-0.0242**	-0.039***	-0.0266*	-0.0233
	γ	-0.312***	-0.12	-0.111**	-0.0716	-0.159***	-0.029	-0.0245
	α	-1.842***	-1.373***	-0.581***	0.108***	0.861***	1.495***	2.038***
Egypt [b]	β_{ds}	0.131	0.119	0.114**	0.00287	0.0782	0.0594	0.106
	δ_{ds}	0.115	0.124	0.0268	0.00291	0.0872	0.188	0.132
	β_{ss}	0.0830**	0.0402	0.0181	-0.00129	-0.0516	-0.016	-0.0443
	δ_{ss}	-0.0423	-0.0344	-0.0512	-0.0013	0.0259	0.0112	0.0273
	β_{rs}	-0.00267	-0.00717	-0.0014	-0.00026	0.0215*	0.0228	0.0201
	δ_{rs}	-0.0503	-0.00973	-0.0180*	-0.00027	-0.0254**	-0.019	-0.0265
	γ	-0.534**	-0.430***	-0.108	-0.00101	-0.173**	-0.341***	-0.496***
	α	-2.353***	-1.378***	-0.413***	0.200***	0.937***	2.040***	2.910***
Greece [b]	β_{ds}	0.518***	0.480***	0.364***	0.326***	0.362***	0.364***	0.329***
	δ_{ds}	-0.0321	0.0784	0.298***	0.221***	0.166**	0.272***	0.273**
	β_{ss}	0.0254	0.000516	-0.0419**	-0.0221	-0.028	-0.0237	-0.0375
	δ_{ss}	-0.041	-0.0377	-0.0447	-0.0614*	-0.0298	-0.0544	-0.015
	β_{rs}	-0.061***	-0.066***	-0.053***	-0.038***	-0.041***	-0.034***	-0.036**
	δ_{rs}	-0.080***	-0.053***	-0.024*	-0.029***	-0.031***	-0.049***	-0.0547**
	γ	-1.615***	-1.240***	-0.541***	-0.0205	0.344***	0.979***	1.356***
	α	-1.917***	-1.362***	-0.618***	0.0658**	0.730***	1.386***	1.835***
Hungary [b]	β_{ds}	0.649***	0.604***	0.534***	0.467***	0.489***	0.493***	0.578***
	δ_{ds}	0.163*	0.131	0.121	0.200***	0.296***	0.384***	0.331**
	β_{ss}	-0.0431	-0.0339	0.00423	-0.0236	-0.0102	-0.042	-0.0476
	δ_{ss}	0.0808	0.0182	-0.07	-0.0709**	-0.0786*	-0.0436	0.000673
	β_{rs}	-0.055***	-0.062***	-0.057***	-0.049***	-0.057***	-0.054***	-0.027
	δ_{rs}	-0.076***	-0.049***	-0.038***	-0.030***	-0.027***	-0.042*	-0.062**
	γ	-0.643***	-0.159	-0.114*	-0.0606	-0.0145	0.115	0.138
	α	-2.207***	-1.787***	-0.782***	0.0837*	1.004***	1.867***	2.513***
Poland [c]	β_{ds}	0.645***	0.631***	0.525***	0.443***	0.428***	0.496***	0.551***
	δ_{ds}	0.00384	0.0247	0.141**	0.278***	0.321***	0.236***	0.176
	β_{ss}	0.0349	-0.0033	-0.0264**	-0.0439**	-0.0446**	-0.0608**	-0.0756*
	δ_{ss}	-0.00205	0.0419	0.0305	0.00965	0.00441	0.0351	0.032
	β_{rs}	-0.072***	-0.075***	-0.068***	-0.063***	-0.055***	-0.061***	-0.047***
	δ_{rs}	-0.056***	-0.0239	-0.0184*	-0.0199**	-0.024***	-0.0176	-0.0376**
	γ	-0.264**	-0.133	-0.0246	0.00697	-0.0827	-0.158*	-0.00487
	α	-2.109***	-1.524***	-0.671***	0.0495	0.868***	1.782***	2.208***

Qatar [a]	β_{ds}	0.0636	0.114	0.0164	0.00202	0.0738*	0.165*	0.076
	δ_{ds}	0.0367	0.0171	0.0484	0.00574	0.0697	-0.0591	0.063
	β_{ss}	0.0458	0.00234	0.00185	-0.00048	-0.0133	0.0331	-0.029
	δ_{ss}	-0.0537	-0.00478	-0.0185	-0.00158	0.00462	-0.057	-0.005
	β_{rs}	0.00776	0.00223	-0.00853	-0.007	-0.0002	-0.003	0.036
	δ_{rs}	-0.050**	-0.043**	-0.0128*	-0.0049	-0.008	0.006	-0.031
	γ	0.088	0.0136	-0.0435	-0.00188	-0.119**	-0.474***	-0.688***
	α	-1.99***	-1.179***	-0.283***	0.0200***	0.530***	1.611***	2.521***
Russia [a]	β_{ds}	0.962***	0.756***	0.714***	0.586***	0.600***	0.701***	0.802***
	δ_{ds}	0.0943	0.286*	0.319***	0.442***	0.431***	0.348***	0.241
	β_{ss}	-0.118	-0.0842	-0.0862**	-0.117***	-0.106***	-0.0672*	-0.0836
	δ_{ss}	0.190*	0.148*	0.142***	0.165***	0.166***	0.095	0.093
	β_{rs}	-0.117***	-0.083***	-0.073***	-0.061***	-0.070***	-0.062***	-0.059***
	δ_{rs}	-0.0049	-0.0428*	-0.040***	-0.042***	-0.034***	-0.0298**	-0.0379
	γ	0.367	0.124	0.0282	-0.197***	-0.214***	-0.232**	0.0508
	α	-3.083***	-1.961***	-0.819***	0.188***	1.105***	2.097***	2.735***
SA [c]	β_{ds}	0.743***	0.673***	0.610***	0.575***	0.564***	0.700***	0.732***
	δ_{ds}	-0.021	0.146	0.237***	0.282***	0.292***	0.131	0.126
	β_{ss}	-0.0248	-0.0274	-0.0473	-0.0500**	-0.076***	-0.0132	-0.0291
	δ_{ss}	0.0798	0.0523	0.0264	0.00756	0.0148	-0.0327	-0.0423
	β_{rs}	-0.103***	-0.109***	-0.085***	-0.072***	-0.065***	-0.062***	-0.062***
	δ_{rs}	-0.00117	0.0117	-0.0169	-0.033***	-0.040***	-0.035***	-0.0286
	γ	0.209	0.189**	0.0538	-0.049	-0.156***	-0.177**	-0.199
	α	-2.200***	-1.601***	-0.717***	0.0941**	0.886***	1.631***	2.205***
Turkey [c]	β_{ds}	0.867***	0.647***	0.521***	0.459***	0.559***	0.612***	0.673***
	δ_{ds}	-0.388	-0.0409	0.109	0.161*	0.0231	-0.121	-0.175
	β_{ss}	-0.00559	0.0548	-0.016	-0.019	-0.0801	-0.0453	-0.133
	δ_{ss}	0.0608	-0.0789	-0.0647	-0.0371	0.0277	0.0297	0.0756
	β_{rs}	-0.166***	-0.136***	-0.104***	-0.091***	-0.082***	-0.062***	-0.020***
	δ_{rs}	0.0364	0.016	0.00806	0.0108	-0.00054	-0.0159	-0.00927
	γ	0.831***	0.446***	0.265**	-0.0499	-0.506***	-0.785***	-1.082***
	α	-3.907***	-2.655***	-1.211***	0.102*	1.520***	2.796***	3.861***
UAE [a]	β_{ds}	-0.0391	0.0388	0.0372	0.00882	0.0228	0.0457	0.098
	δ_{ds}	0.269	0.129	0.0413	-0.00882	0.122*	0.144	0.136
	β_{ss}	0.0885	0.172**	0.0104	-0.00119	-0.0265	-0.0545	-0.0207
	δ_{ss}	-0.130	-0.192**	-0.00959	0.00119	-0.00118	0.00858	-0.0661
	β_{rs}	-0.0084	-0.00615	-0.0059	-0.0058**	-0.00381	0.0306*	0.0536*
	δ_{rs}	-0.061	-0.0461*	-0.0101*	0.0058**	-0.00318	-0.0424**	-0.0494
	γ	1.149***	0.319*	-0.128**	-0.127***	-0.281***	-0.670***	-0.921***
	α	-3.010***	-1.338***	-0.0873*	0.137***	0.624***	1.679***	2.674***
China [c]	β_{ds}	0.042	0.240***	0.164***	0.0231	0.0981*	0.0396	0.0283
	δ_{ds}	0.204	0.0185	0.0278	0.127**	0.102*	0.142	0.253*
	β_{ss}	-0.0641	-0.0610*	0.0147	0.00452	0.00796	-0.00565	-0.00802
	δ_{ss}	0.125	0.065	-0.0438	-0.0215	-0.0287	-0.00888	-0.0164
	β_{rs}	-0.0293	0.00727	0.000369	-0.00128	0.00381	0.00886	0.00593
	δ_{rs}	-0.031	-0.0489**	-0.0262**	-0.00605	-0.0134	-0.00951	-0.00605
	γ	0.139	0.197	0.139**	0.0341	-0.136*	-0.292***	-0.313**
	α	-2.478***	-1.749***	-0.727***	0.0154	0.812***	1.904***	2.584***
India [c]	β_{ds}	0.641***	0.407***	0.290***	0.183***	0.249***	0.339***	0.364***
	δ_{ds}	0.185	0.0423	0.149***	0.233***	0.201***	0.196***	0.18
	β_{ss}	0.0461	-0.0116	-0.0238	-0.0335*	-0.0420**	-0.0298	-0.00155
	δ_{ss}	-0.00013	0.0258	-0.0136	-0.0316	-0.0353	-0.0112	-0.0726
	β_{rs}	-0.0508**	-0.033***	-0.030***	-0.0189**	-0.0213**	-0.0187	-0.0055
	δ_{rs}	-0.0219	-0.0214	-0.032***	-0.037***	-0.031***	-0.0236	-0.0439
	γ	0.407	0.16	0.0147	-0.117***	-0.246***	-0.178*	-0.102
	α	-2.604***	-1.632***	-0.636***	0.142***	0.961***	1.696***	2.246***
Indonesia [c]	β_{ds}	0.546***	0.417***	0.338***	0.174***	0.261***	0.179***	0.374***
	δ_{ds}	-0.213	-0.0651	0.00775	0.141**	0.0745	0.215**	0.0504
	β_{ss}	0.069	0.00152	0.00789	-0.00072	0.0148	-0.00179	0.0452

Country	Param							
Korea [c]	δ_{ss}	-0.0336	-0.0281	-0.0762**	-0.073***	-0.102***	-0.0837**	-0.173**
	β_{rs}	-0.0308	-0.037***	-0.030***	-0.025***	-0.024***	-0.0005	0.00743
	δ_{rs}	-0.0237	-0.0134	-0.0109	-0.0105	-0.0109	-0.0247	-0.038
	γ	0.0582	0.127	0.0858	-0.0869***	-0.186***	-0.278***	-0.352***
	α	-2.366***	-1.620***	-0.672***	0.157***	0.920***	1.775***	2.439***
	β_{ds}	0.266**	0.391***	0.368***	0.252***	0.288***	0.224***	0.113
	δ_{ds}	0.257*	0.0914	0.0857	0.201***	0.212***	0.341***	0.487***
	β_{ss}	-0.0308	-0.0396	0.000287	-0.0343**	-0.00334	0.0215	-0.013
Malaysia [b]	δ_{ss}	-0.0117	0.041	-0.0439	-0.0457***	-0.075***	-0.129***	-0.07
	β_{rs}	-0.0474**	-0.054***	-0.040***	-0.024***	-0.031***	-0.0132	-0.00284
	δ_{rs}	-0.03	-0.0109	-0.00675	-0.034***	-0.022***	-0.0359**	-0.047***
	γ	0.506***	0.403***	0.136*	-0.0123	-0.163***	-0.338***	-0.274**
	α	-2.706***	-1.887***	-0.732***	0.105***	0.909***	1.795***	2.359***
	β_{ds}	0.139*	0.111**	0.0934***	0.0857***	0.137***	0.155***	0.207***
	δ_{ds}	0.100	0.145***	0.181***	0.150***	0.133***	0.131*	0.0881
	β_{ss}	-0.0214	-0.0107	-0.00052	-0.00281	-0.00911	0.0185	0.0239
Pakistan [b]	δ_{ss}	0.0228	0.0193	-0.00305	-0.0103	-0.0138	-0.0266	-0.0532
	β_{rs}	-0.034***	-0.0223**	-0.0114**	-0.010***	-0.00498	-0.00438	-0.00325
	δ_{rs}	-0.00034	-0.0112	-0.018***	-0.016***	-0.022***	-0.0208**	-0.0182
	γ	-0.0405	-0.0282	-0.0495	-0.0168	0.00224	-0.0212	-0.0393
	α	-1.269***	-0.872***	-0.361***	0.0413***	0.451***	0.974***	1.363***
	β_{ds}	0.213	0.235**	0.0363	0.0309	-0.00322	-0.0165	0.0356
	δ_{ds}	-0.242	-0.198*	-0.0171	-0.0263	0.0515	0.131*	0.214
	β_{ss}	0.0307	0.0875	0.0149	-0.0011	-0.0113	-0.0609**	-0.0609
Philippines [b]	δ_{ss}	-0.0479	-0.0984	-0.026	-0.00443	-0.0114	0.0469	0.0291
	β_{rs}	-0.0204	-0.0343	-0.0148	-0.0029	-0.00825	-0.0153	-0.00529
	δ_{rs}	0.0142	0.0254	0.00858	-0.00017	0.00329	0.00985	0.0143
	γ	1.003***	0.591***	0.0246	-0.160***	-0.322***	-0.431***	-0.547***
	α	-2.710***	-1.651***	-0.430***	0.187***	0.898***	1.596***	2.192***
	β_{ds}	0.409***	0.230***	0.149**	0.0710**	0.154***	0.199***	0.216***
	δ_{ds}	-0.260*	-0.053	0.0625	0.0951**	0.0743	0.047	0.0182
	β_{ss}	0.0301	-0.0431	-0.00579	0.000365	-0.0107	-0.0331	-0.0261
Taiwan [c]	δ_{ss}	-0.073	-0.00575	-0.0406	-0.0338*	-0.023	-0.00986	-0.0404
	β_{rs}	-0.0216	-0.0113	-0.00014	-0.0021	-0.00291	-0.00391	-0.0144
	δ_{rs}	-0.0049	-0.0168	-0.0233*	-0.0162**	-0.0159*	-0.0125	0.000127
	γ	0.282*	0.111	0.0637	0.0616*	-0.0948	-0.223***	-0.179*
	α	-2.204***	-1.464***	-0.651***	0.00854	0.802***	1.653***	2.122***
	β_{ds}	0.430***	0.321***	0.181***	0.104***	0.149***	0.254***	0.0878
	δ_{ds}	-0.0892	0.0295	0.0998	0.137***	0.154***	0.0946	0.214
	β_{ss}	0.00437	0.00457	0.00718	-0.0146	-0.0359	-0.0271	-0.0955*
Thailand [c]	δ_{ss}	0.002	-0.0348	-0.0438	-0.0343**	-0.03	-0.0495	0.0359
	β_{rs}	-0.075***	-0.048***	-0.026***	-0.0123	-0.0163*	-0.00928	-0.00663
	δ_{rs}	0.0252	0.00144	-0.0123	-0.0168**	-0.0117	-0.017	-0.00607
	γ	0.507***	0.382***	0.130**	0.0449	-0.195***	-0.303***	-0.392***
	α	-2.398***	-1.609***	-0.648***	0.0193	0.801***	1.560***	2.155***
	β_{ds}	0.377***	0.322***	0.273***	0.180***	0.266***	0.281***	0.196
	δ_{ds}	-0.0328	0.00534	0.0557	0.128***	0.0795*	0.104	0.203
	β_{ss}	0.0706	0.0182	0.0103	-0.0174	-0.026	0.00238	0.0141
	δ_{ss}	-0.109**	-0.0394	-0.0475	-0.0315	-0.0312	-0.0476	-0.0977*
	β_{rs}	-0.036***	-0.0208	-0.021***	-0.010***	-0.0144	-0.0126	0.00714
	δ_{rs}	-0.0205	-0.0288*	-0.021***	-0.022***	-0.0172*	-0.0177	-0.0263
	γ	0.328***	0.246***	0.190***	0.0560**	-0.127**	-0.255***	-0.453***
	α	-2.075***	-1.474***	-0.645***	0.01	0.763***	1.549***	2.195***

Notes: The values report the estimates of the bootstrapped quantile regression results of the following functional form specified in equation (11). The β_{ds}, β_{ss} and β_{rs} represents the quantile coefficients of demand, supply and risk shocks for the full period respectively. Whereas, the δ_{ds}……δ_{rs} denote the quantile coefficients onset the crisis period. The γ parameter captures the marginal intercept value onset the oil price break period. The 10%, 5% and 1% significance levels are denoted by *, ** and *** respectively. [a-] Exporters, [b-] Moderate importers and [c-] Importers

The results of QR analysis are fairly consistent with some previous studies. For instance, Zhu et al., (2016) also find higher tail dependence in the low quantiles for Chinese industry level stocks with respect to change in oil prices. Regarding the statistical pattern of structure and degree of dependence, Hu (2006) also emphasizes that the dependencies across the financial markets is left-tailed and unarguably asymmetric. Moreover, the strong lower-tail sensitivity could also be an outcome of the fact that the influence of oil price shocks is more evident and tractable when markets are bearish than to the situation when the markets are bullish (Zhu et al., 2016). Besides Guo et al., (2018) attributes the heterogenous dependence structure between economic factors and asset prices to the behavioral theories of Barberis et al., (1998) and Lewellen (2002) among others. Thus, the changes in the degree of dependence across the market states could be the consequence of under and over-reaction bias (Guo et al., 2018). Besides, it is also found that onset the GFC the dependence structure has somewhat altered as consistent with former studies (Das et al., 2018b; Zhang et al., 2013). For example, in Figure 11 we plot the β and δ for Russia, additionally the author also plots difference of the slope between β and δ following a similar approach of Baur (2013). As it may be observed, the slope of difference is U-shaped for demand shock, whereas closely S-shaped for supply and risk shocks. Further, it may also be noticed that the difference is heavy at the lower-tails i.e. higher positive values for demand shocks and higher negative values supply and risk shocks. It essentially implies that the lower-tail depict relatively steeper slope for the period onset GFC for Russia. Similarly, we find such differences for other markets as well[47], which indicates that β ≠ δ and hence the dependence structure is inequal. Thus, overall, we find that the dependence structure is affected by the GFC, our finding is similar to Mensi et al., (2014).

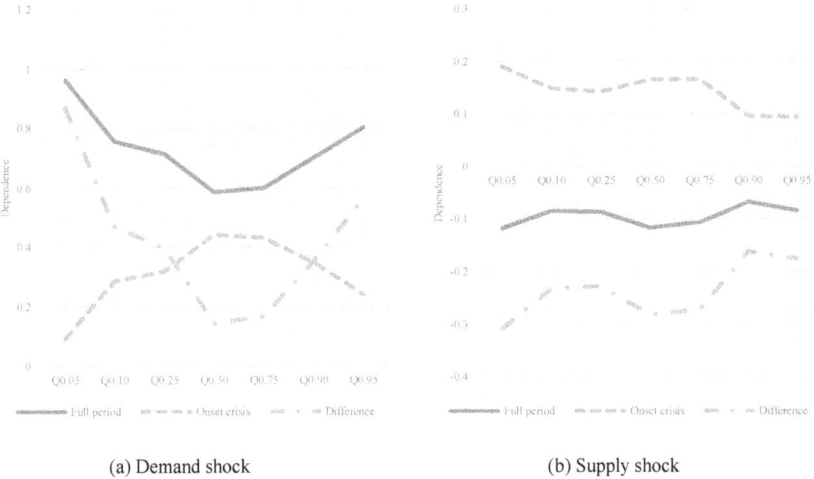

(a) Demand shock (b) Supply shock

---

[47] All the plots β and δ for all the countries are not reported for parsimony.

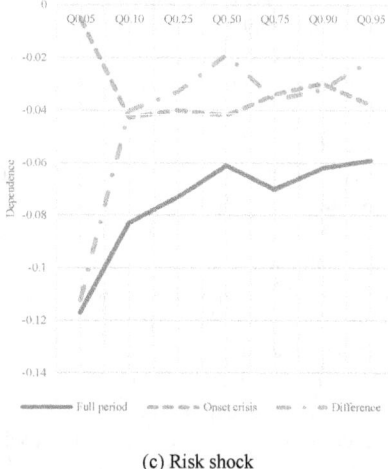

(c) Risk shock

Figure 3.11. Change in degree and structure of dependence for Russia
Notes: The solid blue line represents the QR coefficients for the full-period. The dotted orange-colored line depicts the QR coefficients for the period onset GFC. The grey dash-dotted line denotes the difference between the full and onset crisis period.

3.5. Conclusions

The revisits the relational dynamics of oil price shocks and emerging stock markets to understand the sensitivity of the different markets in response to the shocks. The author uses a sample of 24 emerging equity markets for the period spanning over July 15, 2002 to June 18, 2018 and are bifurcated on the basis of oil-dependence. Further, the author decomposes the oil price changes into shocks using the algorithm suggested recently by Ready (2018). To capture the time-varying co-movements between oil prices and stock returns we use RC and DCC analysis. The regime and state-specific dependence of stock returns on the oil shocks is captured by the MRS and QR models respectively. Overall, the results are consistent with the previous studies. The demand shock is positively associated with stock returns, whereas the supply and risk shocks are mostly negatively associated (Basher et al., 2018; Cunado and de Gracia, 2014; Ready, 2018). However, the do not find strong regime dependent behavior in the MRS model in general. Besides, we also find that the influence of the oil shocks is mostly significant and tractable in the lower tail (bearish markets) in the QR specification, which is consistent with previous studies, *see* (Peng et al., 2017; Reboredo and Ugolini, 2016; Sim and Zhou, 2015; Zhu et al., 2016, 2015). Additionally, the dependence structure is also somewhat altered in the post-GFC era for most of the markets.

One of the notable findings of the , which is worth highlighting is the heterogeneous behavior of stock markets within the oil-dependence groups. For instance, if we focus upon the group of exporters, Colombia and Russia shows positive response to the supply shocks whereas other markets falling in this group depict a negative effect. Similarly, when the focuses upon the group of importers, the author observes that China despite of being the highest importer the negative impact of supply shock is marginal. Whereas, the sensitivity of

India to supply shock is comparatively strong in negative direction (*see* Figure 8). The heterogeneous susceptibility of markets could be attributed to two main conceivable reasons. Firstly, Arouri et al., (2010) explicitly underscores that considerable dispersion exists within the universe of EM in terms of market size, stage of development and market depth. For example, in the present sample set consists of some markets such as Brazil, Indonesia and Turkey which were established in 1877, 1912 and 1866 respectively. At the same, the sample set also includes the countries such as China, where Shanghai and Shenzhen markets were set up relatively recently in 1992. Thus, the different markets may stand at different cyclical phases of the market. Besides, the relevance of market capitalization and the speed of market development could not be negated. Secondly, we must also consider that the present uses the country-specific aggregate stock indexes, however, there could be substantial heterogeneous oil-stock association across the industrial sectors (Arouri et al., 2012). The constituents of the mature markets are usually diversified across the sectors, whereas the constituents could be concentrated for some markets. Thus, the sectorial composition is an indispensable determinant of the oil-stock relationship (Alsalman, 2016; Arouri, 2011; Caporale et al., 2015; Narayan and Sharma, 2011). Thus, the sensitivities depicted by the individual markets to oil price shocks could be an outcome of the sectoral structure of the index.

Table 3.8. Parameter estimates of the bivariate DCC-GARCH (1,1) model

	α	β	α+β	θ_1	θ_2
$N = 4013$					
Brazil [c]	0.0837***	0.8907***	0.9744	0.0152***	0.9834***
Chile [b]	0.1137***	0.8609***	0.9747	0.0215***	0.9733***
Colombia [a]	0.1659***	0.7950***	0.9608	0.0128**	0.9843***
Mexico [a]	0.0964	0.8805***	0.9769	0.0251***	0.9691***
Peru [b]	0.1507***	0.8364***	0.9871	0.0164***	0.9782***
CR [b]	0.0945***	0.8918***	0.9863	0.0126***	0.9844***
Egypt [b]	0.0619	0.9261	0.9879	0.0085	0.9615***
Greece [b]	0.0530	0.9460***	0.9990	0.0146	0.9768***
Hungary [b]	0.0761***	0.9136***	0.9896	0.0132***	0.9830***
Poland [c]	0.0553***	0.9325***	0.9878	0.0171***	0.9799***
Qatar [a]	0.1076***	0.8913***	0.9988	0.0077*	0.9660***
Russia [a]	0.0821***	0.8986***	0.9807	0.0126***	0.9858***
SA [c]	0.0617***	0.9251***	0.9868	0.0204***	0.9748***
Turkey [c]	0.0873***	0.8885***	0.9758	0.0164***	0.9785***
UAE [a]	0.0851***	0.9120***	0.9971	0.0076	0.9709***
China [c]	0.0515	0.9475***	0.9990	0.0217**	0.9317***
India [c]	0.0930***	0.8989***	0.9919	0.0096***	0.9882***
Indonesia [c]	0.1405***	0.8499***	0.9903	0.0237*	0.6155**
Korea [c]	0.0665**	0.9256***	0.9921	0.0127**	0.9764***
Malaysia [b]	0.0635***	0.9308***	0.9943	0.0068***	0.9900***
Pakistan [b]	0.1431***	0.7983***	0.9414	0.0109	0.7789**
Philippines [b]	0.0932***	0.8857***	0.9790	0.0092*	0.9284***
Taiwan [c]	0.0504	0.9427***	0.9931	0.0045*	0.9924***
Thailand [c]	0.1518**	0.8472***	0.9990	0.0033*	0.9952***

Notes: The table exhibits the summary of the bivariate DCC standard GARCH estimates. The DCC parameters α and β captures the effect of the lagged standardized shocks and lagged conditional correlations on the current correlations respectively. The parameters θ_1 and θ_2 represents the mean reverting tendencies of the correlation series. The 10%, 5% and 1% significance levels are denoted by *, ** and *** respectively.

CHAPTER 4

THE ASYMMETRIC OIL PRICE AND POLICY UNCERTAINTY SHOCK EXPOSURE OF EMERGING MARKET SECTORAL EQUITY RETURNS

This essay addresses the third question that is how the oil price and economic policy uncertainty shocks impact the emerging market sectoral equity returns. In addition, the also examines whether the nature of impact is asymmetric in nature. Using the quantile regression analysis, the reports the evidence of asymmetric relationship and more susceptibility of the market in the bearish market state.

4.1. Background

The significant stance of crude oil in world economy has led a rich intellectual base of academic research since the mid of 1970s (Jones et al., 2004). The primitive studies in this field of inquiry delved upon the impact of oil price changes and its macroeconomic consequences upon economic growth and monetary policy besides many other factors (Bruno and Sachs, 1982; Pierce et al., 1974). However, onset the influential work of Hamilton (1983), which documents that oil price shock is a crucial contributor to US economic recession, scholars have investigated several multilateral dimensions on the impact of oil price shocks on the different variables of real economy.[48] Amid of numerous macroeconomic variables, the oil-stock association, in particular, has received utmost importance by scholars and practitioners alike. The prime underlying reason being the stock market movements are the potential precursors to anticipate the changes in economic activities (Fama, 1990). The impact of oil price shocks is expected to stimulate stock prices at least through twin transmission channels. Firstly, we must uphold the fact that oil is an essential industrial input, thus, oil price hike causes thinning of profit margin consequently the stock price is depressed (Apergis and Miller, 2009; Basher and Sadorsky, 2006; Huang et al., 1996; Sadorsky, 1999). Secondly, the increasing oil prices are often regarded as the forerunners of impending inflationary pressures. Thus, the central bankers and policy framers tend to raise the interest rates often to counter the inflationary conditions. Since, the interest rates are used as the discounting factor to price the assets, higher interest rates dampens the intrinsic value of the stocks (Huang et al., 1996; Miller and Ratti, 2009). The oil-stock relationship also claimed its prominence since it owes considerable implications for the investment portfolio management strategies (Basher et al., 2018, 2012; Basher and Sadorsky, 2006; Boyer and Filion, 2007; Jones and Kaul, 1996; Kang and Ratti, 2013; Kayalar et al., 2017; Mohanty et al., 2010; Nandha and Faff, 2008; Park and Ratti, 2008; Ready, 2018).

This essay offers a fresh perspective to the oil-stock relationship in four ways. First, the explicitly focuses upon the role of oil price shocks on the emerging market composite

---

[48] A broad base of literature is evident that enquires impact of oil price shocks on several macroeconomic variables, such as: industrial production and economic activity (Cuñado and de Gracia, 2003; Ewing and Thompson, 2007; Herrera et al., 2011), **monetary policy** (Bernanke et al., 1997; Herrera and Pesavento, 2009; Leduc and Sill, 2004), **inflation** (Cologni and Manera, 2008; Cunado and De Gracia, 2005; Wu and Ni, 2011), **exchange rates** (Atems et al., 2015; Chaudhuri and Daniel, 1998; Chen and Chen, 2007), **commodities** (Chaudhuri, 2001; Pal and Mitra, 2017; Plourde and Watkins, 1998) **and precious metals** (Charlot and Marimoutou, 2014; Hammoudeh and Yuan, 2008; Sari et al., 2010), **beside others.**

sectoral equities. Oil is a crucial commodity in order to foster growth and economic development in the emerging economies. The emerging economies on the cusp of rapid industrialization has demonstrated higher demand for oil (Basher and Sadorsky, 2006; Chattopadhyay and Mitra, 2015; You et al., 2017). Besides, the advanced economies in comparison to the emerging counterparts are more energy efficient on the account of technological innovations and shifting reliance upon renewable energy sources (Basher and Sadorsky, 2006). Thus, higher energy requirements coupled up with heavy oil-dependence exposes emerging economies to oil-price shocks. Consequently, the oil price fluctuations are expected to have intensified impact on the profitability of business firms and asset prices in emerging economies (Basher and Sadorsky, 2006). The precedence of vulnerabilities in emerging economies in response to oil price rise can be traced back to the event of the oil embargo levied by Organization of Petroleum Exporting Countries (OPEC) in 1973. The embargo imposition by OPEC caused a steep rise in oil prices from 3 to 13 US dollars per barrel. Consequently, a critical upsurge in oil importing costs was witnessed for the emerging economies leading social and economic hardships (Basher and Sadorsky, 2006). To rescue the emerging economies amid such a crisis, World Bank (WB) and International Monetary Fund (IMF) intermediated to provide financial aid so that the economic developmental projects remain uninterrupted in these economies (Rifkin, 2003). However, such borrowings of the emerging economies led to severe consequences when the commercial bank debts surged by 550% during 1973-1980. Besides, the subsequent oil shock of 1979, which originated a global recession, distressed the emerging economies further since the export prices fell and oil import prices escalated. By the year 1985, the quantum of debt to the Third World countries surpassed 1 trillion US dollars (Basher and Sadorsky, 2006). As a result, these economies resorted to a debt-trap, where new financial loans were being borrowed to service the existing debts and to import oil. The residual funds were inadequate to fund the developmental projects (Basher and Sadorsky, 2006).

Thus, the severity and far reaching implications of oil prices on emerging economies could clearly be understood. Such a concern motivated the financial economists and practitioners to undertake research studies upon the oil-stock relationship in emerging economies (*see* Asteriou and Bashmakova, 2013; Basher et al., 2012; Basher and Sadorsky, 2006; Bhar and Nikolova, 2010; Ghosh and Kanjilal, 2016; Mohanty et al., 2010; Narayan and Narayan, 2010; You et al., 2017; Zhu et al., 2016 among others). The previous studies that include emerging markets in their sample set mostly consider the country or region-specific aggregate equity indexes (Aloui et al., 2012; Basher et al., 2018, 2012; Basher and Sadorsky, 2006; Fayyad and Daly, 2011; Gil-Alana and Yaya, 2014; Masih et al., 2011; Mensi et al., 2016, 2014; Ramos and Veiga, 2013). One of the crucial limitations of examining the oil-stock relationship using aggregate stock index is the understatement of heterogeneity of relationship across the industrial sectors (Arouri et al., 2012). Thus, it is imperative to understand the dynamics of the sectoral stocks and oil in the context of emerging markets. Though there are some studies that focusses upon the oil-sectoral stock relationship, however, those are majorly concentrated and confined to the Chinese context (Caporale et al., 2015; Cong et al., 2008; Li et al., 2012; Peng et al., 2017; Xiao et al., 2018; You et al., 2017; Zhu et al., 2016, 2015). In this concern, Smyth and Narayan (2018) clearly underscores the fact that except for China, the studies regarding the other transition or emerging markets are limited. Besides, they also argue that there is an immense need for sector-based studies considering broad country samples. In this article, we consider the 11 composite emerging market sectoral indexes constructed by Morgan Stanley Capital International (MSCI), which encapsulates 25 emerging equity markets.[49] Thus, we believe our enriches the existing literature by offering a holistic understanding of emerging market sectoral equity behavior in response to oil shocks.

Second, the majority of the previous studies focusing on the oil-stock relationship is constrained by one common limitation. The studies either ignore to decompose the oil price changes into demand and supply shocks or the decomposition is done using the algorithm of Kilian (2009), for instance, (*see* Abhyankar et al., 2013; Aggarwal et al., 2012; Ajmi et al., 2014; Apergis and Miller, 2009; Basher et al., 2018, 2012; Basher and Sadorsky, 2006; Broadstock et al., 2012; Broadstock and Filis, 2014; Nusair and Al-Khasawneh, 2017; Nusair and Olson, 2018; Peng et al., 2017; Wang et al., 2013; You et al., 2017; Zhu et al., 2016, 2015 among others). To develop an in-depth understanding of oil price and stock market dynamics, it is indispensable to recognize the source from which the shock originates i.e. whether demand or supply side shock. The demand shock is related to oil price rise due to higher demand. The demand shock is expected to be positively associated with stock prices. The fundamental reason being demand for oil tend to rise with the advent of country's economic growth and higher consumption propensity by public at large, which incentivizes the firms to produce more. The supply shock, on the other hand, is related with rise in oil prices due to the higher cost pressures in the oil extraction and production process. The supply shocks are expected to negatively affect the stock prices since oil is seldom substitutive as an industrial input. The higher input costs are lively to erode the profit margin of the firms and hence depress earnings and stock prices. Moreover, the expectation of oil price uncertainties may also force the firms to postpone any further new revenue generating investments (Bernanke, 1983). Thus, it is essential to understand the sensitivity of stock prices to either nature of oil shock. Kilian's (2009) work addresses this crucial issue and proposes the oil shock decomposition algorithm, which is widely used in subsequent empirical investigations and in varied contexts, for example (*see* Basher et al., 2018; Jadidzadeh and Serletis, 2017; Kang et al., 2015; Wang et al., 2013, among others). Nevertheless, nearly after a decade, Ready (2018) highlights some significant shortcomings of the Kilian's (2009) shock decomposition procedure and recommends a substitute algorithm that presumably overcomes the existing inadequacies.[50] Hence, we use the measure of Ready (2018) to decompose the oil price shocks for the purpose of our .

Third, the recent studies posit that the oil-stock relationship is not established in seclusion from Economic Policy Uncertainty (EPU) (Kang et al., 2017; Kang and Ratti, 2013; You et al., 2017). The studies fundamentally argue that the oil shocks and EPU are somewhat interrelated and have joint influence over the stock returns. It must be noted that the oil price shocks lead to changes in the level of inflation, real incomes and relative prices (Kang and Ratti, 2013). These changes have considerable influence on the aggregate economy and are often of paramount concern for the producers, consumers and policy makers. In this regard, the previous studies argue that oil shocks engender a trade-off between rising inflation and low output stabilization, which is often a matter of apprehension for the policy makers (Montoro, 2012; Natal, 2012). The adverse effect of oil price shocks is transmitted to the economic activities through the channels of fiscal or monetary policies implemented by the state in response to such shocks (Bernanke et al., 2004; Pieschacón, 2012). Thus, there is a certain joint

---

[49] The sectoral index details are provided in Section 3.1. which describes the data. The 25 markets as per the MSCI emerging market classification dated December 19, 2018 are: Brazil, Chile, Colombia, Mexico, Peru, Czech Republic, Egypt, Greece, Hungary, Poland, Qatar, Russia, South Africa, Turkey, United Arab Emirates, Saudi Arabia, China, India, Indonesia, Korea, Malaysia, Pakistan, Philippines, Taiwan and Thailand.

[50] We discuss the fundamental differences between the process of oil shock computation of Kilian (2009) and Ready (2018) in Section 3, which is devoted to discussion of methodological approach. We clearly highlight the benefits of using the computing procedure suggested by Ready (2018) over the other.

influence of oil shocks and EPU over stock returns. Though a growing literature is focussing upon the impact of EPU on stocks (Anderson et al., 2009; Bekaert et al., 2009; Brogaard and Detzel, 2015; Das and Kumar, 2018; Guo et al., 2018; Mensi et al., 2014; Pastor and Veronesi, 2012), the literature considering both oil and EPU shocks is limited despite of its economic significance (Smyth and Narayan, 2018). Thus, we consider the impact of EPU along with oil shocks upon the stock returns.[51]

Fourth, You et al., (2017) argue that the studies that consider both oil and EPU to assess its impact over the stock returns are few (albeit extremely relevant) (*see* Arouri et al., 2014; Kang et al., 2017; Kang and Ratti, 2015, 2013). The studies, however, largely overlook the distributional heterogeneity which is inherent to the stock returns and the non-linear effect of oil price shocks are not taken into consideration (You et al., 2017). In this regard, Reboredo and Ugolini (2016) states that the market reactions to oil shocks are complex and are essentially determined by the state of the market i.e. whether the market is bearish or bullish. Similar observations are also documented in the respect of EPU by previous studies (Chang et al., 2015; Guo et al., 2018; Mensi et al., 2014; You et al., 2017). Thus, in order to capture the impact of oil and EPU shocks on the stock returns, we resort to quantile regression approach. This approach describes the impact of the predictor variables upon the entire conditional distribution of the predicted variable. Therefore, the quantile-based approach is now a recognized econometric technique in analyzing the oil-stock relationship (Lee and Zeng, 2011; Nusair and Al-Khasawneh, 2017; Nusair and Olson, 2018; Sim and Zhou, 2015; Xiao et al., 2018; You et al., 2017; Zhu et al., 2016, 2015). Additionally, we also examine the asymmetric impact of high and low oil and EPU shocks on the stocks returns across the quantiles. The underlying motivation is the fact that the influence of exogenous shocks on the real economic or financial variables could be asymmetric. For instance, Mork (1989) and Mork et al., (1994) in their respective studies assert that the oil price rise has a definite negative influence on the Gross Domestic Product (GDP). However, a fall in oil prices may not necessarily have a positive impulse on GDP or an impulse equivalent to the case of oil price rise. We endeavor to examine such asymmetric behavior in the context of oil and EPU in relation to stock returns.[52] Unquestionably, the asymmetric exposure of stock returns is respect of oil and EPU shocks is imperative for devising portfolio and risk management strategies.

4.2. Literature Review

In this segment the author briefly discusses the key strands of literature congruent with the primary objective of our in addition to a concise introductory review on the oil-stock relationship.[53] Oil is one of the most important and scarce natural resources, which is inevitable for the growth and development of modern economy. Onset the major oil shock in 1970s that led macroeconomic and political severities, a plethora of studies investigate the relationship between oil price shocks and several economic/financial variables. Hamilton (1983) documents

---

[51] The earlier studies of Kang et al., (2017) and Kang and Ratti (2013) use a vector autoregression framework to examine the relationship between stock returns with oil shocks and EPU. However, our approach is somewhat similar to You et al., (2017), their investigates the impact of oil shocks and EPU on Chinese sectoral equity returns using quantile regression framework.

[52] Some prior studies investigate and confirm the asymmetric oil-stock relationship, for instance, (*see* Cong et al., 2008; Nusair and Al-Khasawneh, 2017; Nusair and Olson, 2018; Park and Ratti, 2008; Ramos and Veiga, 2013; Reboredo and Ugolini, 2016; Tsai, 2015; You et al., 2017 among others).

[53] The readers may refer Smyth and Narayan (2018) for a detailed literature review on the relationship of oil prices and stock returns. In addition the readers are also requested to refer Chapter 3, literature review section, for a brief discussion of the other stands of literature.

that oil price shocks are the harbingers of inflationary conditions in the US. Besides, Fang and You (2014) also argue that the influence of oil price shocks is disseminated to the economy through several transmission channels, such as real balance, income transfer and allocation channels. Amongst all other macroeconomic variables, the relationship between oil and stock has been a matter of interest in both academia and practice alike. The stock prices are commonly viewed as the bellwethers of an economy and the oil price shocks are expected to have potential impact on stock index movements. The findings of the existing literature are diverse, contextual (oil-stock relationship may be different for oil-importing and exporting countries) and inconclusive.

The literature affirms a negative association between oil price changes and stock returns. The negative association is postulated based on the cash-flow hypothesis.[54] As we have mentioned earlier, since oil is an essential industrial input for most of the business firms, soaring oil prices are likely to erode the profit margin. Hence, the quantum of cash inflows to the firm is curtailed which further causes fall in stock prices. In addition, the rising oil prices emit signals of imminent inflationary conditions which prompts the central bankers and other governing authorities to scale up the interest rates as a counter remedial measure. Since, the interest rates are used as the discounting factor to value the stocks, the higher interest rates cause diminution of intrinsic value. Thus, oil price rise could have a potential negative influence upon the stock prices (Cunado and de Gracia, 2014; Filis and Chatziantoniou, 2014; Jones and Kaul, 1996; Mensi et al., 2017; Park and Ratti, 2008; Sadorsky, 1999). In contrast, few studies also report the evidences of positive response of stock returns in respect to changes in oil prices (Chen and Lv, 2015; El-Sharif et al., 2005; Sadorsky, 2001; Zhu et al., 2016). In this context, Kollias et al., (2013) argue that the possible positive oil-stock relationship could be an artefact of a booming economy. As the economy fosters growth and industrial development, the demand for oil increases. Consequently, the demand-side pressures drive up the oil prices. Thus, the augmented consumption propensity on the wake of economic growth incentivizes the firms to produce and sell more unit of products to match the demand. The increased sales volume generates higher profits and hence stock prices tend to upsurge. We discuss some more categorical dimensions of oil-stock relationship as below:

4.2.1. Oil prices and emerging economies

Basher and Sadorsky (2006) highlight the greater vulnerabilities of emerging markets to oil shocks as compared to the developed economies on account of higher oil-dependence to fuel the process of economic growth. However, the studies concerning the oil-stock relationship in emerging economies are inadequate and deserves further attention (Smyth and Narayan, 2018). Nonetheless, growing literature examining the oil-stock association in China is clearly evident owing to their increasing oil consumption and high oil import growth (Caporale et al., 2015; Cong et al., 2008; Ding et al., 2017; Kang and Ratti, 2015; Li et al., 2017, 2012; Xiao et al., 2018; You et al., 2017; Zhu et al., 2016, 2015). Similarly, some limited continent and country-specific studies concerning emerging economies can be traced in the literature, for instance, in African continent (Gil-Alana and Yaya, 2014; Gupta and Modise, 2013; Lin et al., 2014), **Central and Eastern Europe** (Asteriou and Bashmakova, 2013; Mohanty et al., 2010), **Gulf Co-operation Council** (Hammoudeh and Aleisa, 2004; Maghyereh and Al-Kandari, 2007; Mohanty et al., 2018; Nusair and Al-Khasawneh, 2017), **India** (Ghosh and

---

[54] The cash flow hypothesis states that the value of any financial asset is determined by the expected future cash inflows after discounting at a certain rate (Fisher, 1930; Williams, 1938) i.e. $V_i = E(CF)/E(r)$. Where, V_i is value of the asset i, $E(.)$ is the expectation operator and CF and r are the expected future cash inflows and discount rate respectively.

Kanjilal, 2016; Tiwari et al., 2018), **Russia** (Bhar and Nikolova, 2010) and **Vietnam** (Narayan and Narayan, 2010) among others. Several other studies consider group of emerging economies to investigate the oil-stock association (Aloui et al., 2012; Basher et al., 2018, 2012; Basher and Sadorsky, 2006; Dogah and Premaratne, 2018; Gupta, 2016; Nasir et al., 2018; Ramos and Veiga, 2013; Zhu et al., 2017). Nevertheless, within the universe of scarce literature on the oil-stock relationship in emerging economies, the studies focussing upon sectoral equity responses in relation to oil shocks is further limited. Though some of the recent literature recognize the gap attempt to bridge this issue (Dogah and Premaratne, 2018; Tiwari et al., 2018; Xiao et al., 2018; You et al., 2017; Zhu et al., 2016, 2015), there remains a considerable scope for undertaking further investigations. Thus, in our we consider the composite emerging market sectoral equity returns to examine its behaviour in response to the oil price shocks.

4.2.2. Oil prices and sectoral equity returns

As we mention above, the majority of the studies regarding the oil-stock relationship in emerging economies consider the aggregate stock indexes (Aloui et al., 2012; Basher et al., 2012; Basher and Sadorsky, 2006; Dutta et al., 2017; Zhu et al., 2017). Considering the aggregate indexes invite a crucial limitation on the estimates oil-stock association. Arouri et al., (2012) argue that considering the aggregate stock index returns potentially conceal the market-wide heterogeneous impact of oil shocks across the sectors. The markets which are mature are more diversified across many sectors, however, the sectorial spread for the markets which are presently at an embryonic stage are concentrated in few industries (Smyth and Narayan, 2018). Besides, Narayan and Sharma (2011) assert that the different sectors have a different market structure thus the impact of oil shocks on the stocks is likely to be distinct. It must be noted that the degree to which the sector is vulnerable to oil shocks depend upon the fact that whether oil serves as the input or output to the sector (Mohanty et al., 2018). Moreover, the magnitude of oil shock's impact on stock returns is expected to be determined by degree of concentration, competition in the particular sector. Additionally, the inherent abilities of the sectors to transfer or absorb the oil price changes also determine the sensitivity of its stocks towards oil shocks (Arouri and Nguyen, 2010). For example, the oil and gas sector stocks in general is positively related to oil price changes (Boyer and Filion, 2007; Cong et al., 2008; Gupta, 2016; Li et al., 2017; Nandha and Faff, 2008; Sadorsky, 2001). Whereas, the sector related to the consumer goods is negatively associated to oil price changes (Ready, 2018). The prior studies confirm that the sensitivity to oil shocks vary substantially across the sectors (Broadstock and Filis, 2014; Degiannakis et al., 2013; Elyasiani et al., 2011; Gogineni, 2010; Mohanty et al., 2011; Nandha and Brooks, 2009; Narayan and Sharma, 2011). Thus, the overall estimated relationship between oil and stock considering the aggregate stock indexes could be biased since the relationship is largely driven by sectorial composition (Alsalman, 2016; Arouri, 2011; Narayan and Sharma, 2011). However, despite the crucial importance of the sector-specific investigations, the studies are largely concentrated in the context of developed economies. For example, US (Elyasiani et al., 2011; Narayan and Sharma, 2011), Europe (Arouri and Nguyen, 2010; Moya-Martínez et al., 2014; Xu, 2015), the G7 group of countries (Lee et al., 2012). In the emerging markets perspective, abundant sector-based studies are available in the context of China (Caporale et al., 2015; Cong et al., 2008; Li et al., 2017, 2012; Peng et al., 2017; Xiao et al., 2018; You et al., 2017; Zhu et al., 2016, 2015). Nevertheless, the sector-specific studies in emerging markets apart from China is limited (Smyth and Narayan, 2018). Thus, there occurs a need to undertake further investigations upon the oil-stock relationship in emerging markets.

4.3. Data and Methodology

4.3.1. Data description

The dataset comprises of 11 composite emerging market sectors classified by the MSCI. The sectors are: consumer discretionary (CD), consumer staples (CS), energy (EY), financials (FN), health care (HC), industrials (IN), information technology (IT), materials (MT), real estate (RE), telecommunications (TL) and utilities (UT). We consider the dollarized daily closing index prices of each sector and the data is extracted from the Bloomberg database. The period of ranges from December 30, 1994 to November 23, 2018 enveloping 6236 daily observations. To decompose the oil price changes into the demand, supply and risk driven shocks using the algorithm of Ready (2018), we have considered three additional variables. The first variable is the stock price index of the oil and gas producing firms. We use the MSCI All Country World Index (ACWI) Energy Index for this purpose.[55] The third variable is the oil price changes proxied by 1-month returns on NYMEX -Light Sweet Oil contracts. Further, to understand the role of US-based policy uncertainties on emerging markets sectoral equity returns we consider the US EPU index constructed by Baker et al., (2016).[56] The innovations in the EPU index is similarly estimated as of VIX.

In addition, we consider five control variables, first is the Standard and Poor's 500 index (S&P500) of US stock market to control for the movement of the global stocks and investment conditions, following past studies, *see* Mensi et al., (2014). Second, the role of exchange rate has been considered pivotal by previous studies to understand the oil-stock relationship since the crude oil is priced in US dollars (*see* Aloui et al., 2012; Basher and Sadorsky, 2006; Basher et al., 2012; Xiao et al., 2018; You et al., 2017). Thus, we use the Trade-Weighted Exchange Rate (TWEX) index, which is the weighted average foreign exchange values of the US dollar against the major US trading partner currencies similar to the preceding studies (Aloui et al., 2012; Basher and Sadorsky, 2006; Basher et al., 2012; Ferson and Harvey, 1994).[57] Third, we also consider the gold prices as an essential control variable on

---

[55] The readers are requested to refer Chapter 3, data description section, for the details of ACWI index and its constituents.

[56] The policy related uncertainties of US is commonly viewed and considered as a proxy for global uncertainty (*see* Das and Kumar, 2018; Ko and Lee, 2015). Moreover, we could not use the data for Global EPU since it is available only in monthly frequency. For the brief discussion of index construction methodology of EPU, the readers are requested to refer Chapter 2, data section.

[57] We use the Federal Reserve Board's Broad Trade-Weighted Exchange Rate index (TWEXBMTH). This index comprises of the weighted average US dollar exchange values of broad currency group of major trading partners with US. The index envelopes the currencies of Euro Area, Canada, Japan, Mexico, China, United Kingdom, Taiwan, Korea, Singapore, Hong Kong, Malaysia, Brazil, Switzerland, Thailand, Philippines, Australia, Indonesia, India, Israel, Saudi Arabia, Russia, Sweden, Argentina, Venezuela, Chile and Colombia. The index broadly covers both developed and emerging economy currencies. The major currencies of the advanced economies that are traded in liquid financial markets can be used to assess financial market pressures bearing upon the US dollar (Basher et al., 2012). Though, it is true that there are only few currencies globally, the trading volume of which is influential enough to move foreign exchanges and oil markets (Basher et al., 2012), however the increasing trade-dependence of US on emerging economies such as China, Mexico, South Korea and India may also not be negated (*see* https://www.forbes.com/sites/kenroberts/2018/02/28/top-10-u-s-trade-partners-in-2017-can-be-broken-into-three-tiers/#8c63d59627e8, accessed December 13, 2018; 18:10 Hours, IST). Thus, we

two counts: (a) the emerging markets are largely commodity-dependent, some of the major emerging markets such as India, China, South Korea, Thailand are major gold consumers in the world, whereas South Africa is one of the major gold producers in the world (Mensi et al., 2014; Wen and Cheng, 2018). Thus, the gold price fluctuations are expected to have significant influence upon the stock prices of emerging markets. (b) The emerging markets are traditionally being considered as the potential avenues for international portfolio diversification since the notable work of Grubel (1968) and Levy and Sarnat (1970). However, with growing market integration across the world the emerging markets are now exposed to various macroeconomic risk spills from the developed markets. Gold being a safe-haven asset (Baur and Lucey, 2010; Baur and McDermott, 2010) may be preferred by the investors over the emerging markets during the events of economic turbulences -a flight to safety phenomenon. Thus, there could be a possible interaction between gold and emerging markets.

In addition to the other factors mentioned above the possibility of market turmoil (or the economic crises) plaguing the oil-stock relationship cannot be negated (You et al., 2017). Chen and Lv (2015) for instance, reports that the extremal dependence between oil and Chinese stock market increase intensely during the period of crisis i.e. contagion effect. Nonetheless, the dependence between oil and stocks tranquilize after the crisis. Similarly, Luo and Quin (2017) also emphasizes the role of economic crisis in determining the oil-stock association. Thus, we account for two noteworthy financial crises events using dummy variable that is expected to have impending repercussions on the oil-stock relationship following a similar approach of Nusair and Al-Khasawneh (2017) and Nusair and Olson (2018). The first vector of dummies corresponds to the Asian Financial Crisis (AFC) that prevails over July 1997 to December 1998, the second vector controls for the Global Financial Crisis (GFC) for the period starting from March 2008 till September 2009.[58] The vectors takes the value of 1 during the crisis period, 0 otherwise.

4.3.2. Methodology

Our methodological approach is dual-faceted. Firstly, to decompose the oil price shocks into demand shock, supply shock and risk shock, we use the Vector Autoregression (VAR) type process suggested recently by Ready (2018).[59] Secondly, in order to understand the response of stock prices to the oil prices shocks across the different market states we use the quantile regression analysis.

4.3.2.1. Quantile regression

We examine the asymmetric impacts of oil price shocks and EPU innovations on the emerging market sectoral equity returns at the different market conditions. Our baseline regression equation that also incorporates the probable influences of the control variables may be expressed as follows:

$$r_{i,t} = \alpha + \beta_1 ds_t + \beta_2 ss_t + \beta_3 rs_t + \beta_4 epus_t + \beta_5 sp500_t + \beta_6 twex_t + \beta_7 gold_t + \beta_8 d\_AFC_t + \beta_9 d\_GFC_t + \varepsilon_t$$

---

consider the Broad Trade-Weighted Exchange Rate index, which considers both developed and emerging economy currencies. Higher values of TWEX index depict stronger US dollars.
[58] The crisis dates are similarly specified as by Demirer et al., (2018).
[59] For the discussion on the shock decomposition procedure of Ready (2018), readers are requested to refer the Chapter 3, methodology section.

(1)

where r_t denotes the emerging market sectoral equity returns at time t for sector i. The ds_t, ss_t and rs_t signifies the demand, supply and risk shocks respectively at time t. The $epus_t$ stands for the EPU shocks at time t. The rest are the control variables S&P500 index, TWEX, Gold at time t. The vectors of crisis dummies are noted by d_AFC_t and d_GFC_t. The equation (1) makes an assumption that the impacts of oil price and EPU shocks on equity returns are symmetrical. Thus, the specified model cannot evaluate the asymmetric impact of high and low oil and EPU shocks on equity returns. To address this potential shortcoming of equation (4), we modify the specification as below:

$$r_{i,t} = \alpha + \beta_{11} ds_t^{(+)} + \beta_{12} ds_t^{(-)} + \beta_{21} ss_t^{(+)} + \beta_{22} ss_t^{(-)} + \beta_{31} rs_t^{(+)} + \beta_{32} rs_t^{(-)} + \beta_{41} epus_t^{(+)} + \beta_{42} epus_t^{(-)} + \beta_5 sp500_t + \beta_6 twex_t + \beta_7 gold_t + \beta_8 d\_AFC_t + \beta_9 d\_GFC_t + \varepsilon_t$$
(2)

where

$$ds_t^{(+)} = max(ds_t, 0), and\ ds_t^{(-)} = min(ds_t, 0)$$
$$ss_t^{(+)} = max(ss_t, 0), and\ ss_t^{(-)} = min(ss_t, 0)$$
$$rs_t^{(+)} = max(rs_t, 0), and\ rs_t^{(-)} = min(rs_t, 0)$$
$$epus_t^{(+)} = max(epus_t, 0), and\ epus_t^{(-)} = min(epus_t, 0)$$

It should be noted that equations (1) and (2) are capable to capture only the average effects of oil and EPU shocks on stock returns. The stock markets, in general, oscillates across different market conditions such as bearish, normal and bullish states. Thus, it is imperative for investors and policy makers to understand how the oil and EPU shocks impact the stock returns at different market conditions in order to device appropriate risk management strategy. In such a situation, the quantile regression technique proposed by Koenker and Bassett (1978) could serve as an effective estimation procedure since it can capture the impact of the independent variables at the different conditional distributions of the dependent variable. In addition, in comparison to the Ordinary Least Square (OLS) regression, the quantile regression is capable of producing more precise results since it is less susceptible to the outlier observations, skewness of the distribution and heterogeneity on the dependent variable (Koenker & Hallock, 2001).

Let us consider y to be the dependent variable which is linearly dependent on the variable x. In such a case, the τth conditional quantile of y may be expressed as:

$$Q_y(\tau|x) = \sum_k \beta_k(\tau) x_k = x'\beta(\tau)$$
(3)

where, the dynamic dependence relationship between the τth conditional quantile of y and the vector of x is given by the QR coefficient $\beta(\tau)$. The dependence is held to be conditional if the exogeneous variables are added to x, and unconditional otherwise. The complete dependence structure of y is determined by the values of $\beta(\tau)$ for $\tau \in [0,1]$. Thus, on the basis of the specific explanatory variable contained in the vector of x, there could be four prime nature of dependence structure: (a) $\beta(\tau)$ decreases (increases) corresponding to the values of τ (i.e. monotonic), (b) $\beta(\tau)$ is unchanged at different values of τ (i.e. constant), (c) $\beta(\tau)$ is similar at higher and lower quantiles (i.e. symmetric) and (d) $\beta(\tau)$ is dissimilar at higher and lower quantiles (i.e. asymmetric).

For a given τ, the coefficients $\beta(\tau)$ are estimated by a minimization process of the weighted absolute deviations between y and x, which is expressed as:

$$\hat{\beta}(\tau) = \arg\min \sum_{t=1}^{T}\left(\tau - 1_{\{y_t < x_t'\beta(\tau)\}}\right)|y_t - x_t'\beta(\tau)| \qquad (4)$$

where, the indicator function is expressed as $1_{\{y_t < x_t'\beta(\tau)\}}$. The solution to the minimization problem stated above is achieved by using the linear programming algorithm proposed by Koenker and D'Orey (1987). We use the pair bootstrapping procedure suggested by Buchinsky (1995) to obtain the standard errors of the estimated coefficients. The derived standard errors are asymptotically valid under the conditions of misspecification and heteroscedasticity of the QR function. The QR model is specified to investigate the heterogeneous impact of conditioning variables (i.e. the oil price and EPU shocks) on the quantile function of stock returns, equations (1) and (2) is transformed as:

$$Q_{r_{i,t}}(\tau|x) = \alpha(\tau) + \beta_1(\tau)ds_t + \beta_2(\tau)ss_t + \beta_3(\tau)rs_t + \beta_4(\tau)epus_t + \beta_5(\tau)sp500_t + \beta_6(\tau)twex_t + \beta_7(\tau)gold_t + \beta_8(\tau)d\_AFC_t + \beta_9(\tau)d\_GFC_t + \varepsilon_t \qquad (5)$$

$$Q_{r_{i,t}}(\tau|x) = \alpha(\tau) + \beta_{11}(\tau)ds_t^{(+)} + \beta_{12}(\tau)ds_t^{(-)} + \beta_{21}(\tau)ss_t^{(+)} + \beta_{22}(\tau)ss_t^{(-)} + \beta_{31}(\tau)rs_t^{(+)} + \beta_{32}(\tau)rs_t^{(-)} + \beta_{41}(\tau)epus_t^{(+)} + \beta_{42}(\tau)epus_t^{(-)} + \beta_5(\tau)sp500_t + \beta_6(\tau)twex_t + \beta_7(\tau)gold_t + \beta_8(\tau)d\_AFC_t + \beta_9(\tau)d\_GFC_t + \varepsilon_t \qquad (6)$$

We report the coefficient values of seven quantiles as regression output in the results section, namely, $\tau = (0.05, 0.10, 0.25, 0.50, 0.75, 0.90$ and $0.95)$. The low quantiles $(0.05, 0.10, 0.25)$ designate the bearish, the median quantile, (0.50) denote the normal and finally, higher quantiles $(0.75, 0.90, 0.95)$ signify bullish market condition.

4.4. Empirical Results

The Figure 1 exhibit the time trends of the aggregate emerging market (EM) index[60], oil prices (NYMEX), oil producers index (ACWI Energy index), VIX, EPU, TWEX and gold. It can be clearly observed that the emerging market index depict plummeting tendencies during the crisis periods that are shaded in grey color. The oil prices and oil producers index clearly collapse around the year 2007-08, which corresponds to the period of GFC. Unprecedented spikes could be observed for the VIX around this period, alongside the EPU index also show high uncertainties. Further, the exchange rate (TWEX) also weakens during this period, nevertheless, the gold prices soar up when all other asset depict dwindling tendencies. Baur and Lucey (2010) and Baur and McDermott (2010) refer this phenomenon as the safe-haven property of gold. Table 1 reports the descriptive statistics of the variables under consideration. The highest mean returns are observed for the Health Care (HC) sector, whereas the lowest returns are observed for Real Estate (RE) sector. The highest volatile (stable) sector (in terms of standard deviation) is Energy (Consumer Staples (CS)) among all the sectors. The returns for all the sectors during the period of is negatively skewed. It essentially means more frequent occurrences of negative returns than the positive ones. In addition, the excess kurtosis is observed for all the sectoral series. Hence, the skewness-kurtosis (S-K) test clearly shows that the data series is non-normal, which motivate us to use the quantile regression analysis for examining the relational dynamics. Lastly, we report the Augmented Dickey-Fuller (ADF) and Philipps-Perron (PP) test statistics to confirm that all the series are stationary.

---

[60] We do not plot all the sectoral series for parsimony.

Table 2 reports the estimation results of the quantile regression for the specification in Equation (8) in addition to the OLS results for Equation (4), to facilitate a comparative analysis. The OLS regression reports the average impact of the predictor variables upon the predicted variables (Xiao et al., 2018; Zhu et al., 2016). The β_1 represents the coefficient for the demand shocks and it shows a statistically significant and positive relationship with the aggregate emerging market as well as for all other sectors, with only exception to the industrials sector (IN). Ready (2018) suggests that the demand shocks are associated with rise in oil prices due to higher demand for oil, besides Kollias et al., (2013) also states that higher demand for oil could be driven by a state of booming economy. Thus, the need for higher quantum of production could propel the need for higher demand for oil. The higher production in turn is expected to generate high cash flows to the firms at the micro level, which further leads to higher stock prices. Thus, our results are consistent with the theoretical connotations. The coefficient for the industrials sector (IN) is negative, however, weak and statistically insignificant.

The coefficients of supply shock as reported by β_2 depict a statistically significant and negative association with stock returns for the aggregate emerging markets index and also across all the sectoral equity returns. As we mention before, the supply shocks signify the rise in oil prices due to the supply-side cost pressures. The higher input cost for the firms reduces the profit margin and hence a negative relationship is expected theoretically. Our results are congruent with the theoretical predictions. Similarly, the innovations in VIX reported by β_3 is significantly negative for all the variables. It is not surprising, since the VIX is also referred as the investor's fear gauge (Whaley, 2000). Thus, an innovation in VIX is expected to signal potential fall in the stock markets and hence the stocks may tend to fall. The EPU coefficients represented by β_4 illustrate a mixed impact across all the sectors. The coefficients are weak, negative and insignificant for some sectors (EM, CD, CS, FN, MT, UT), negative and significant for some (HC, IN, IT and RE) and weakly positive and insignificant for the rest of the sectors (EY, TL). The baseline expectation of negative EPU and stock relationship is somewhat fulfilled, however, the direction and magnitude of impact is heterogenous across the sectors.

In addition, the coefficients of the control variables are reported in β_5 to β_9. The S&P500 index coefficients reported by β_5 indicate a positive and significant relationship for most of the sectors and aggregate emerging market index. An insignificant positive relationship is observed for the sectors EY and IT. The relationship is also significantly negative for RE and insignificantly negative for HC and IN sectors. A negative relationship between the developed and emerging markets is often appreciated and sought after for international portfolio diversification. Furthermore, the TWEX and gold represented by β_6 and β_7 respectively mostly show a negative association. Lastly, the dummy variables reported by the coefficients β_8 and β_9 majorly show a significant negative relationship for AFC and a significant positive relationship for GFC, with few marginal exceptions. The plausible reason being the fact that during the AFC the funds started flowing out from the emerging markets and the developed markets in US and Europe witnessed substantial capital inflows (Van Wincoop and Yi, 2000). Thus, the AFC could essentially be attributed as the emerging market crisis (Demirer et al., 2018). Nevertheless, the GFC dummy mostly shows positive coefficients suggesting a reverse situation to AFC.

In comparison to the OLS regression, the quantile regression is a better technique since it can captivate the impact of oil and EPU shocks on returns at the various market conditions. Thus, the relationship between oil, EPU and stock returns could be examined in a more comprehensive manner. Thus, we use the Equation (8) and perform the quantile regression analysis and the results are reported in Table 2, columns 3-9. Withstanding the results of the OLS regression, the coefficient β_1 in respect of the demand shocks, clearly show a positive and significant relationship across all the quantiles for the aggregate emerging markets index and also for the sectors. The supply and risk shocks depicted by β_2 and β_3 also shows significant negative association across the market states. The impact of the EPU shock denoted by β_4 is mostly negative, however, somewhat inconsistent and weak. Further, overall, we find that the impact of these variables on returns is profound under the bearish market conditions. Though this finding is of some interest, however, we are not the first to report such a phenomenon. Similar results were reported by some previous studies that investigates the oil-stock relationship (*see* Xiao et al., 2018; Zhu et al., 2016 among others). Regarding the statistical pattern of structure and degree of dependence, Hu (2006) also emphasizes that the dependencies across the financial markets is left-tailed and unarguably asymmetric. Moreover, the strong lower-tail sensitivity could also be an outcome of the fact that the influence of oil price shocks is more evident and tractable when markets are bearish than to the situation when the markets are bullish (Zhu et al., 2016). Besides Guo et al., (2018) attributes the heterogenous dependence structure between economic factors and asset prices to the behavioural theories of Barberis et al., (1998) and Lewellen (2002) among others. Additionally, we also report the results for the equality of the slopes test across the quantiles in Table 3. The null hypothesis of this test suggests the coefficients have the similar slope across the quantiles. For parsimony we report the results for one median (0.50) and high (0.95) quantile against a low quantile (0.05). The results clearly suggest the rejection of null hypothesis in all the case with minor exceptions.

We clearly find the evidence that the oil and EPU shocks has considerable influence on the emerging market sectoral equity returns. In the next step, we examine the asymmetric exposure of these sectoral indexes following the methodological approach some previous studies (Nusair and Al-Khasawneh, 2017; Nusair and Olson, 2018; Xiao et al., 2018; You et al., 2017). Therefore, we decompose the oil and EPU shocks into positive and negative changes and examine their impact on the equity returns based on the specification in Equation (5) and (9). The positive oil and EPU shock changes denote the increase in oil prices and policy uncertainties and vice-versa. The Table 4 reports the estimation results of the quantile regression analysis in addition to the results of OLS regression. The coefficients of the control variables are not reported to save space. Overall, we report an interesting phenomenon. We find that unquestionably the demand shocks positively impact the stock returns, however, the negative demand stocks have stronger positive impact on stock returns than the positive demand shocks. On the other hand, the stock returns are more vulnerable to supply and risk shocks when the shocks are positive than negative. Similar is the case of the EPU shocks, however, some significant and positive coefficients could be observed. The underlying reason could be attributed to the fact that in the case of the US based policy uncertainties the investors might shift their investments from US to emerging markets. Thus, boosting the emerging markets and generating the positive impact. The difference of coefficients has been substantiated by using the Wald test, where the null hypothesis is $H_0: \beta_{X1} = \beta_{X2}$. We reject the null hypothesis in most of the cases indicating an asymmetric relationship among the variables. Further, we also report the equality of slope test across the quantiles in Table 5, we clearly observe that the null hypothesis is rejected in the case of most of the sectors and we conclude that the relationship is asymmetric. Finally, we plot the coefficient of the quantile regression specified in Equation (9) for the aggregate emerging markets index to show the behaviour of the coefficients across the quantiles.

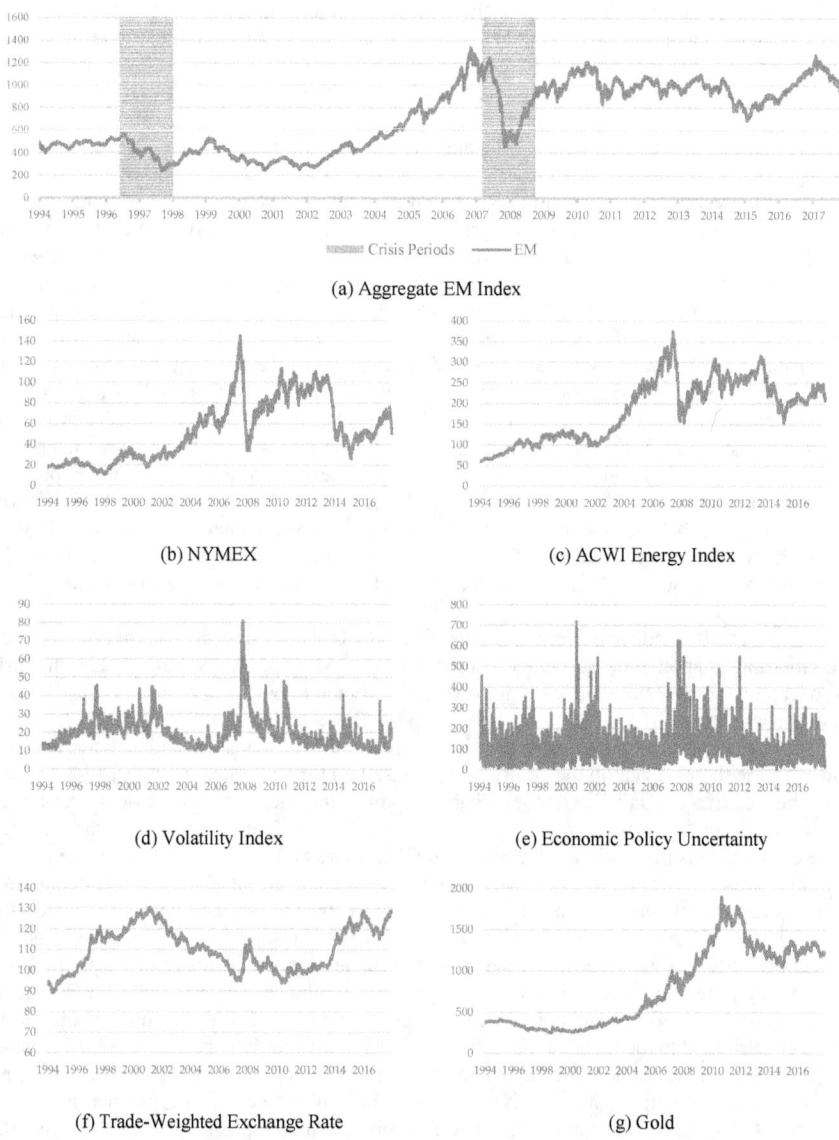

Figure 4.1. Time-trends of indexes
Note: The indexes are expressed in US dollars (with exception to EPU). All data are extracted from Bloomberg.

Table 4.1. Descriptive statistics

	Mean	Std. Dev.	Maximum	Minimum	Skewness	Kurtosis	S-K Test	ADF	PP
EM	0.011	1.161	10.073	-9.995	-0.530	10.696	0.000***	-62.095***	-61.653***
CD	0.015	1.288	9.675	-10.183	-0.354	8.413	0.000***	-64.134***	-63.677***
CS	0.021	0.956	7.671	-8.263	-0.626	9.629	0.000***	-63.925***	-63.446***
EY	0.020	1.594	16.066	-14.880	-0.442	12.312	0.000***	-65.048***	-64.532***
FN	0.012	1.248	10.151	-9.186	-0.380	9.368	0.000***	-63.737***	-63.475***
HC	0.032	1.134	6.402	-6.908	-0.271	6.365	0.000***	-73.819***	-73.660***
IN	-0.009	1.249	10.740	-11.512	-0.623	11.847	0.000***	-63.845***	-63.884***
IT	0.025	1.557	12.185	-9.888	-0.189	6.115	0.000***	-68.649***	-68.484***
MT	0.007	1.324	10.188	-13.080	-0.524	11.990	0.000***	-61.249***	-60.855***
RE	-0.018	1.507	10.092	-9.318	-0.104	7.324	0.000***	-64.656***	-64.432***
TL	0.007	1.264	10.228	-10.135	-0.164	9.977	0.000***	-65.347***	-64.722***
UT	0.002	1.294	10.966	-9.808	-0.343	10.549	0.000***	-64.946***	-65.375***
SP500	0.029	1.142	10.957	-9.470	-0.264	11.878	0.000***	-84.286***	-85.062***
NYMEX	0.017	2.300	16.410	-16.545	-0.073	7.338	0.000***	-80.641***	-80.780***
ACWI Energy	0.020	1.303	12.277	-13.362	-0.504	12.413	0.000***	-70.515***	-70.081***
VIX	0.008	6.497	76.825	-35.059	0.897	10.044	0.000***	-84.806***	-87.973***
EPU	-0.024	63.420	321.562	-314.833	0.053	4.110	0.000***	-122.025***	-207.669***
TWEX	0.005	0.321	1.947	-2.280	0.212	6.761	0.000***	-82.577***	-82.554***
Gold	0.019	1.021	10.245	-9.512	-0.076	10.811	0.000***	-80.056***	-80.049***
Demand Shock	0.000#	1.128	10.102	-10.924	-0.141	11.048	0.000***	-71.447***	-71.092***
Supply Shock	-0.000#	2.024	18.697	-17.008	0.040	8.741	0.000***	-83.425***	-83.868***
Risk Shock	0.008	6.457	78.594	-32.048	1.027	10.453	0.000***	-78.547***	-79.466***

Notes: EM- MSCI Emerging Market Index. S-K test stands for the Skewness-Kurtosis test for normality. S-K test is similar to the Jarque-Bera (JB) (1987) test, i.e. it is also calculated from the sample Skewness and Kurtosis. Nonetheless, we must note that the JB test is based on the asymptotic standard errors without sample size corrections. Whereas, the S-K test incorporates two adjustments for sample size suggested by Royston (1992) and D'Agostino et al., (1990). We report the *p*-values of the S-K test. *** indicate significance at 1% level. # Only first three decimal values has been reported.

Table 4.2. Estimation results for oil and EPU shocks with controls

		0.05	0.10	0.25	0.50	0.75	0.90	0.95	OLS
EM	β_1	0.338***	0.285***	0.312***	0.290***	0.296***	0.257***	0.205***	0.324***
	β_2	-0.0107	-0.0231	-0.0258***	-0.0269***	-0.0342***	-0.0187**	-0.0134	-0.0241***
	β_3	-0.0792***	-0.0596***	-0.0488***	-0.0438***	-0.0379***	-0.0264***	-0.0209***	-0.0489***
	β_4	-0.00203***	-0.000508	-0.000441	-3.68E-05	0.000348	0.000156	0.000408	-0.000225
	β_5	-0.000563	0.0897*	0.0890***	0.0977***	0.132***	0.183***	0.257***	0.0945***
	β_6	-1.031***	-0.937***	-0.783***	-0.766***	-0.792***	-0.857***	-1.021***	-0.938***
	β_7	0.0227	0.00466	0.018	-0.0131	-0.00992	-0.0193	-0.0182	-0.0151
	β_8	-0.784***	-0.674***	-0.276***	-0.0786	0.0352	0.159	0.324**	-0.154***
	β_9	-0.730***	-0.586***	-0.262***	0.032	0.304***	0.601***	0.811***	0.0248**
CD	β_1	0.313***	0.247***	0.221***	0.227***	0.224***	0.207***	0.220***	0.256***
	β_2	0.0123	-0.00348	-0.0191**	-0.0227***	-0.0224***	-0.00978	0.0062	-0.0160**
	β_3	-0.0759***	-0.0587***	-0.0470***	-0.0413***	-0.0314***	-0.0212***	-0.0253**	-0.0463***
	β_4	-0.00191***	-0.00106*	-0.000573***	-0.000228	0.000263	0.000545	0.00102*	-0.000196
	β_5	-0.0113	0.0566	0.134***	0.140***	0.169***	0.254***	0.239**	0.121***
	β_6	-1.039***	-1.045***	-0.861***	-0.896***	-0.981***	-1.129***	-1.189***	-1.030***
	β_7	0.00301	-0.00187	-0.0141	-0.0428**	-0.0428**	-0.0621***	-0.131***	-0.0411***
	β_8	-0.839***	-0.466***	-0.342***	-0.151**	-0.0464	0.122	0.417**	-0.188***
	β_9	-0.899***	-0.451**	-0.143	0.0339	0.370***	0.631***	0.837***	0.0280*
CS	β_1	0.261***	0.233***	0.219***	0.215***	0.202***	0.185***	0.169***	0.227***
	β_2	-0.00591	-0.00866	-0.0261***	-0.0217***	-0.0201***	-0.0254***	-0.0250**	-0.0190***
	β_3	-0.0604***	-0.0524***	-0.0440***	-0.0340***	-0.0281***	-0.0216***	-0.0202***	-0.0399***
	β_4	-0.00108	-0.000694***	-0.000159	-0.000107	0.000328*	0.000508***	0.00119**	-7.47E-05
	β_5	0.0241	0.0529	0.0812***	0.115***	0.130***	0.188***	0.217***	0.102***
	β_6	-0.989***	-0.880***	-0.754***	-0.734***	-0.762***	-0.793***	-0.869***	-0.847***
	β_7	-0.00349	-0.017	-0.00906	-0.00635	-0.0184	-0.0171	-0.0416**	-0.0180*
	β_8	-0.834***	-0.503***	-0.241***	-0.0112	0.102**	0.179**	0.466***	-0.0984***
	β_9	-0.399*	-0.251**	-0.121***	0.0543	0.138**	0.321***	0.291***	0.0293***
EY	β_1	0.569***	0.609***	0.627***	0.646***	0.608***	0.602***	0.602***	0.638***
	β_2	-0.0079	-0.0128	-0.0242***	-0.0249***	-0.0153**	-0.0215*	-0.0151	-0.0157**
	β_3	-0.102***	-0.0923***	-0.0734***	-0.0730***	-0.0602***	-0.0572***	-0.0540***	-0.0761***
	β_4	-0.000982	0.000239	-0.000204	-0.000101	0.000278	0.000624	0.000776	1.97E-05
	β_5	-0.033	-0.00959	0.0146	0.00231	0.0768***	0.112**	0.185**	0.0359
	β_6	-0.998***	-0.862***	-0.725***	-0.686***	-0.733***	-0.768***	-0.788***	-0.879***
	β_7	0.0213	0.0209	-0.00169	-0.0175	-0.0303	-0.0129	0.0085	-0.0219
	β_8	-1.648***	-1.328***	-0.565***	-0.126	0.296**	0.810***	1.195***	-0.216***
	β_9	-0.962***	-0.762***	-0.331***	0.0468	0.359***	0.544***	0.825***	0.0410**

		(1)	(2)	(3)	(4)	(5)	(6)	(7)	(8)
FN	β_1	0.375***	0.326***	0.317***	0.279***	0.283***	0.234***	0.221***	0.330***
	β_2	-0.0234*	-0.0294***	-0.0303***	-0.0271***	-0.0430***	-0.0191	-0.0207	-0.0280***
	β_3	-0.0812***	-0.0668***	-0.0508***	-0.0420***	-0.0373***	-0.0198**	-0.0178**	-0.0501***
	β_4	-0.00251***	-0.00128***	-0.000628**	-0.000111	0.000155	0.000790***	0.00167***	-0.00038
	β_5	-0.109**	-0.0163	0.0489	0.0801***	0.103***	0.209***	0.197***	0.0437**
	β_6	-1.198***	-1.045***	-0.856***	-0.857***	-0.908***	-1.018***	-1.175***	-1.031***
	β_7	-0.049	-0.0131	-0.00397	-0.0235	-0.0267	-0.0326	-0.0676***	-0.0408***
	β_8	-0.983***	-0.716***	-0.323***	-0.0757	0.0687	0.374***	0.453***	-0.138**
	β_9	-1.287***	-1.141***	-0.311**	-0.0019	0.433***	1.051***	1.365***	-0.00371
HC	β_1	0.187***	0.203***	0.170***	0.151***	0.130***	0.0871***	0.0489	0.158***
	β_2	-0.03	-0.0195	-0.0172**	-0.0240***	-0.0211**	-0.00963	-0.00999	-0.0206***
	β_3	-0.0689***	-0.0510***	-0.0372***	-0.0296***	-0.0258***	-0.0105	-0.00684	-0.0337***
	β_4	-0.00176***	-0.00169***	-0.000479*	-0.000219	-0.000243	0.000213	0.000488	-0.000474**
	β_5	-0.122	-0.0657	-0.0043	0.0103	0.0207	0.0799**	0.0599	-0.0109
	β_6	-0.627***	-0.529***	-0.630***	-0.552***	-0.647***	-0.763***	-0.789***	-0.621***
	β_7	0.00664	0.0227	0.00594	-0.00851	-0.0392**	-0.0648***	-0.0971***	-0.0211
	β_8	-0.382*	-0.263	-0.062	-0.0182	-0.00175	-0.0915	-0.287	-0.0977*
	β_9	-0.489***	-0.278***	-0.115	0.0174	0.0824	0.197**	0.234	0.0427***
IN	β_1	0.333***	0.291***	0.273***	0.245***	0.235***	0.252***	0.267***	-0.00170
	β_2	-0.00876	-0.0184	-0.0278***	-0.0270***	-0.0306***	-0.0340***	-0.0316	-0.0290***
	β_3	-0.0819***	-0.0570***	-0.0444***	-0.0361***	-0.0315***	-0.0314***	-0.0255***	-0.0489***
	β_4	-0.00311***	-0.00174***	-0.000793***	-0.000182	0.000251	0.000118	0.000775	-0.000690***
	β_5	-0.157**	-0.0293	0.0194	0.0606***	0.0539	0.047	0.0927***	-0.0177
	β_6	-1.050***	-0.904***	-0.757***	-0.750***	-0.809***	-0.956***	-1.090***	-0.945***
	β_7	-0.0577*	-0.0358	-0.0241	-0.0275**	-0.0408***	-0.0757***	-0.0666***	-0.0534***
	β_8	-0.941***	-0.847***	-0.467***	-0.230**	0.0642	0.232**	0.402**	-0.222**
	β_9	-2.010***	-1.404***	-0.497***	0.0159	0.508***	0.849***	1.577***	-0.0778
IT	β_1	0.275***	0.248***	0.214***	0.137***	0.125***	0.105**	0.0918	0.165***
	β_2	0.0124	-0.0177	-0.0310**	-0.0276***	-0.0223	-0.0164	-0.00627	-0.0223**
	β_3	-0.0727***	-0.0513***	-0.0432***	-0.0283***	-0.0246***	-0.0113	0.0122	-0.0353***
	β_4	-0.00337***	-0.00203***	-0.000954***	-0.000353	-0.000152	-0.000631	-0.00098	-0.000791**
	β_5	-0.148**	-0.0608***	0.00374	0.0434	0.0832**	0.162**	0.267***	0.0375
	β_6	-0.920***	-0.757***	-0.731***	-0.620***	-0.771***	-0.797***	-0.985***	-0.817***
	β_7	-0.0895	-0.0992*	-0.0569**	-0.0299	-0.0517**	-0.0365	-0.0421	-0.0596***
	β_8	-1.047***	-1.078***	-0.410***	-0.182**	0.316***	0.996***	0.910***	-0.0972
	β_9	-1.105***	-0.845***	-0.281***	0.0774	0.424***	0.671***	0.841***	0.0359*
MT	β_1	0.451***	0.437***	0.385***	0.390***	0.383***	0.373***	0.363***	0.437***
	β_2	-0.0225	-0.0279***	-0.0268***	-0.0268***	-0.0261***	-0.0223*	-0.0404***	-0.0299***
	β_3	-0.0853***	-0.0703***	-0.0536***	-0.0517***	-0.0497***	-0.0382***	-0.0345***	-0.0590***

RE								
β_4	-0.00152***	-0.000774***	-0.000332	-0.000205	5.38E-05	0.000514	0.0006	-0.000256
β_5	-0.0408	0.0677	0.134***	0.122***	0.150***	0.210***	0.221***	0.101***
β_6	-1.223***	-1.081***	-0.905***	-0.923***	-0.934***	-0.995***	-1.054***	-1.073***
β_7	0.0919***	0.109***	0.105***	0.0901***	0.103***	0.0888***	0.115***	0.0811***
β_8	-0.420**	-0.330***	-0.147**	-0.107**	-0.0998**	-0.0721	-0.188**	-0.148***
β_9	-1.268***	-0.830***	-0.312**	0.0755	0.258***	0.565***	0.832***	-0.0363
β_1	0.373***	0.260***	0.229***	0.236***	0.263***	0.234***	0.242***	0.309***
β_2	-0.0275*	-0.0102	-0.0242**	-0.0307***	-0.0360***	-0.0466***	-0.0645***	-0.0323***
β_3	-0.0828***	-0.0442***	-0.0372***	-0.0331***	-0.0414***	-0.0348***	-0.0201***	-0.0474***
TL								
β_4	-0.00286***	-0.00115*	-0.000684	-0.000359	-4.74E-05	-0.000584	-0.000213	-0.000635***
β_5	-0.232***	-0.0634	-0.0271	0.00417	-0.0461	-0.00277	0.0541	-0.0770***
β_6	-0.927***	-0.997***	-0.783***	-0.764***	-0.855***	-0.968***	-1.114***	-0.929***
β_7	-0.0408	-0.0148	-0.0134	-0.0359*	-0.0222	-0.0534	-0.0708	-0.0516***
β_8	-1.410***	-1.231***	-0.802***	-0.143*	0.12	0.718***	1.018***	-0.252***
β_9	-1.939***	-1.552***	-0.879***	-0.162	0.755***	1.450***	2.110***	-0.0803
β_1	0.246***	0.228***	0.227***	0.214***	0.188***	0.152***	0.135***	0.205***
β_2	0.0228	-0.0105	-0.0259***	-0.0407***	-0.0403***	-0.0330*	-0.0305	-0.0232***
β_3	-0.0628***	-0.0498***	-0.0379***	-0.0272***	-0.0222***	-0.0103	-0.00824	-0.0318***
UT								
β_4	-0.000626	0.000206	0.000202	0.000195	0.000514*	0.000349	0.000145	0.000254
β_5	0.219***	0.229***	0.248***	0.258***	0.291***	0.385***	0.423***	0.301***
β_6	-0.931***	-0.872***	-0.678***	-0.603***	-0.698***	-0.769***	-0.873***	-0.786***
β_7	0.0381	0.0309	-0.009	0.00788	-0.0102	-0.0166	0.0159	0.00463
β_8	-1.174***	-1.060***	-0.405**	-0.0453	0.320***	0.616***	0.821***	-0.135**
β_9	-0.678***	-0.371**	-0.235***	-0.0216	0.187**	0.332***	0.621***	-0.0408
β_1	0.314***	0.254***	0.261***	0.276***	0.260***	0.249***	0.189***	0.280***
β_2	-0.0322***	-0.0359***	-0.0479***	-0.0501***	-0.0274***	-0.0105	-0.0199	-0.0404***
β_3	-0.0866***	-0.0619***	-0.0462***	-0.0386***	-0.0305***	-0.0333***	-0.0234***	-0.0468***
β_4	-0.000163	-0.000680***	-0.000196	-7.83E-05	5.69E-05	0.000144	-0.000173	-0.000181
β_5	-0.0358	0.0708	0.0931***	0.112***	0.155***	0.155***	0.250***	0.127***
β_6	-1.117***	-0.956***	-0.734***	-0.655***	-0.689***	-0.752***	-0.766***	-0.849***
β_7	0.0514	0.0446**	0.00592	-0.00196	-0.000353	-0.0448***	-0.0222	-0.00622
β_8	-2.044***	-1.746***	-0.823***	-0.12	0.386**	0.942***	1.615***	-0.211***
β_0	-0.278	-0.220***	-0.142	0.0539	0.178***	0.163***	0.308***	0.00891

Note: The estimation results are reported for Equation (4) and (8). The 10%, 5% and 1% significance levels are denoted by *, ** and *** respectively.

Table 4.3. Quantile slope equality for oil and EPU shocks

		0.05 against the other quantiles				0.05 against the other quantiles	
		0.50	0.95			0.50	0.95
EM	β_1	2.09**	4.07***	IN	β_1	1.85*	1.01
	β_2	1.96**	0.17		β_2	1.15	1.06
	β_3	-4.67***	-5.41***		β_3	-4.23***	-4.04***
	β_4	-4.01***	-3.14***		β_4	-4.31***	-3.58***
CD	β_1	2.21**	1.34	IT	β_1	1.74*	2.41**
	β_2	1.65	0.24		β_2	2.08**	0.58
	β_3	-4.42***	-4.41***		β_3	-2.32**	-4.33***
	β_4	-2.38**	-2.97***		β_4	-3.32***	-1.93*
CS	β_1	1.41	2.55**	MT	β_1	1.59	1.57
	β_2	1.35	1.17		β_2	0.30	1.03
	β_3	-3.75***	-5.36***		β_3	-4.43***	-4.52***
	β_4	-1.58	-2.59***		β_4	-2.44**	-3.94***
EY	β_1	-1.75	-0.50	RE	β_1	2.42**	1.67
	β_2	0.64	0.20		β_2	0.18	1.68*
	β_3	-1.97**	-2.44**		β_3	-5.22***	-4.69***
	β_4	-0.87	-1.60		β_4	-3.04***	-1.76*
FN	β_1	3.14***	2.88***	TL	β_1	0.69	1.95*
	β_2	0.27	-0.13		β_2	3.63***	2.22**
	β_3	-5.62***	-5.89***		β_3	-4.08***	-4.54***
	β_4	-7.01***	-5.71***		β_4	-1.55	-1.06
HC	β_1	1.34	3.02***	UT	β_1	1.31	3.25***
	β_2	-0.35	-0.75		β_2	1.01	-0.60
	β_3	-3.62***	-4.38***		β_3	-5.86***	-6.50***
	β_4	-2.17**	-2.44**		β_4	-0.11	0.01

Note: The 10%, 5% and 1% significance levels are denoted by *, ** and *** respectively.

Table 4. 4. Estimation results for positive and negative oil and EPU shocks with controls

		0.05	0.10	0.25	0.50	0.75	0.90	0.95	OLS
EM	β_{11}	0.069	0.0959**	0.163***	0.271***	0.360***	0.434***	0.493***	0.305***
	β_{12}	0.702***	0.610***	0.465***	0.306***	0.227***	0.0822***	-0.00883	0.338***
	$H_0: \beta_{11} = \beta_{12}$	-4.55***	-6.67***	-5.17***	-0.81	2.61***	3.74***	6.58***	-1.07
	β_{21}	-0.0639*	-0.0682***	-0.0456***	-0.0329***	-0.0143	0.0225	0.0341	-0.0302***
	β_{22}	0.0402	0.0183	-0.0135	-0.0152	-0.0510***	-0.0515***	-0.0378	-0.0187*
	$H_0: \beta_{21} = \beta_{22}$	-2.00***	-2.53**	-1.14	-0.86	1.42	1.84*	1.24	-0.69
	β_{31}	-0.117***	-0.0817***	-0.0606***	-0.0513***	-0.0409***	-0.0310***	-0.0236***	-0.0572***
	β_{32}	-0.0448***	-0.0380***	-0.0359***	-0.0323***	-0.0363***	-0.0234***	-0.0218**	-0.0362***
	$H_0: \beta_{31} = \beta_{32}$	-3.10***	-4.04***	-3.04***	-2.49**	-0.82	-0.75	-0.18	-3.93***
	β_{41}	3.39E-05	-5.62E-05	-0.000241	0.000293	3.43E-06	-0.000728	-0.0018	-0.000386
	β_{42}	-0.00157**	-0.000595	-0.000698	-0.000235	0.000678	0.00103*	0.00216***	5.51e-06
	$H_0: \beta_{41} = \beta_{42}$	0.89	0.50	0.62	1.00	-0.87	-1.47	-2.91***	-0.57
CD	β_{11}	0.0197	0.0375	0.0881***	0.173***	0.287***	0.383***	0.516***	0.230***
	β_{12}	0.617***	0.539***	0.379***	0.268***	0.157***	0.0957	-0.0155	0.277***
	$H_0: \beta_{11} = \beta_{12}$	-4.88***	-5.90***	-5.71***	-1.88*	2.16**	2.13**	4.14***	-1.28
	β_{21}	-0.0782***	-0.0534	-0.0462***	-0.0258***	-0.00527	0.0522**	0.0890*	-0.0196
	β_{22}	0.0897***	0.0516	0.000892	-0.0196	-0.0344**	-0.0746**	-0.0741**	-0.0132
	$H_0: \beta_{21} = \beta_{22}$	-2.18**	-1.77*	-1.50	-0.30	1.15	2.44**	2.30**	-0.33
	β_{31}	-0.113***	-0.0857***	-0.0591***	-0.0485***	-0.0311***	-0.0266**	-0.0212**	-0.0541***
	β_{32}	-0.0368***	-0.0352***	-0.0305***	-0.0309***	-0.0319***	-0.0239**	-0.0285***	-0.0341***
	$H_0: \beta_{31} = \beta_{32}$	-4.35***	-3.81***	-2.80***	-2.13**	0.07	-0.16	0.47	-3.15***
	β_{41}	-0.00164	-0.000592	-0.000526	-0.00029	-0.000614	-0.00109	0.000891	-0.000675
	β_{42}	-0.00233**	-0.000749	-0.000741	-0.000236	0.000905*	0.00219***	0.00217***	0.000344
	$H_0: \beta_{41} = \beta_{42}$	0.38	0.08	0.18	-0.07	-1.66	-2.01**	-0.58	-1.24
CS	β_{11}	0.0374	0.0799**	0.147***	0.187***	0.261***	0.313***	0.354***	0.209***
	β_{12}	0.502***	0.385***	0.294***	0.233***	0.139***	0.0625**	0.051	0.240***
	$H_0: \beta_{11} = \beta_{12}$	-4.37***	-4.14***	-4.83***	-1.44	2.92***	5.21***	3.81***	-1.23
	β_{21}	-0.0647***	-0.0660***	-0.0365***	-0.0241***	-0.0151	0.00696	0.00275	-0.0264***
	β_{22}	0.0460***	0.0328	-0.0132	-0.0166*	-0.0249**	-0.0550***	-0.0431**	-0.0122
	$H_0: \beta_{21} = \beta_{22}$	-2.84***	-2.14**	-1.16	-0.52	0.56	2.12**	1.15	-1.05
	β_{31}	-0.0776***	-0.0665***	-0.0564***	-0.0378***	-0.0274***	-0.0238***	-0.0264***	-0.0444***
	β_{32}	-0.0333***	-0.0338***	-0.0335***	-0.0258***	-0.0256***	-0.0312***	-0.0401***	-0.0325***
	$H_0: \beta_{31} = \beta_{32}$	-2.58***	-3.22***	-3.09***	-2.40***	-0.36	1.84*	1.55	-2.72***
	β_{41}	-0.00254**	-0.000413	-0.000317	0.000344	0.000389	-0.000248	0.000101	-0.000180

		(1)	(2)	(3)	(4)	(5)	(6)	(7)	(8)
EY	β_{42}	4.29E-05	-7.00E-05	-9.62E-05	-0.000374	0.000301	0.000744	0.00152***	7.19e-05
	$H_0: \beta_{41}=\beta_{42}$	-1.75*	-0.32	-0.31	1.49	0.17	-1.00	-1.37	-0.44
	β_{11}	0.133**	0.304***	0.426***	0.629***	0.774***	0.886***	0.982***	0.630***
	β_{12}	1.135***	0.935***	0.810***	0.665***	0.486***	0.375***	0.195***	0.644***
	$H_0: \beta_{11}=\beta_{12}$	-6.06***	-7.61***	-6.92***	-0.39	3.48***	5.23***	4.75***	-0.34
	β_{21}	-0.113**	-0.0834**	-0.0669***	-0.0122	0.000943	0.0472	0.0637*	-0.0276**
	β_{22}	0.0366	0.0353**	0.0297	-0.0272***	-0.0422***	-0.0711**	-0.0860**	-0.00421
	$H_0: \beta_{21}=\beta_{22}$	-1.81*	-2.71***	-3.14***	0.51	1.95**	2.24**	2.64***	-1.06
	β_{31}	-0.152***	-0.123***	-0.0806***	-0.0725***	-0.0635***	-0.0549***	-0.0512***	-0.0809***
	β_{32}	-0.0818***	-0.0807***	-0.0652***	-0.0707***	-0.0663***	-0.0771***	-0.0730***	-0.0686***
	$H_0: \beta_{31}=\beta_{32}$	-2.21**	-4.15***	-1.85*	-0.24	0.27	1.53	1.14	-1.72*
	β_{41}	-0.00159	-0.000351	0.000446	0.00053	0.0011	0.000449	0.000347	0.000205
	β_{42}	0.00105	0.000702	-6.58E-05	-0.000598	-0.000508	0.00058	0.000612	-0.000119
FN	$H_0: \beta_{41}=\beta_{42}$	-1.03	-0.57	0.46	1.04	1.46	-0.10	-0.17	0.35
	β_{11}	0.0626	0.0564	0.197***	0.238***	0.386***	0.459***	0.549***	0.315***
	β_{12}	0.715***	0.669***	0.479***	0.327***	0.178***	0.0306	0.00433	0.340***
	$H_0: \beta_{11}=\beta_{12}$	-5.24***	-6.78***	-3.15***	-1.80*	3.52***	5.54***	5.08***	-0.74
	β_{21}	-0.0647***	-0.0568***	-0.0642***	-0.0360**	-0.0207	0.00522	0.0593***	-0.0368***
	β_{22}	0.033	0.00901	-0.0121	-0.0136	-0.0589***	-0.0610**	-0.0663***	-0.0198*
	$H_0: \beta_{21}=\beta_{22}$	-1.89*	-2.52**	-2.26**	-0.76	0.99	1.18	2.85***	-0.91
	β_{31}	-0.0998***	-0.0820***	-0.0680***	-0.0508***	-0.0393***	-0.0287**	-0.0366***	-0.0576***
	β_{32}	-0.0621***	-0.0418***	-0.0356***	-0.0359***	-0.0345***	-0.0175	-0.0216**	-0.0386***
	$H_0: \beta_{31}=\beta_{32}$	-3.32***	-3.53***	-3.77***	-2.52**	-0.48	-0.78	-0.80	-3.15***
	β_{41}	-0.000757	-0.000619	-4.51E-05	0.000157	-0.000266	-0.000893	-0.000512	-0.000427
	β_{42}	-0.00235**	-0.00169**	-0.000745	-0.000351	0.00036	0.00209***	0.00214***	-0.000269
HC	$H_0: \beta_{41}=\beta_{42}$	0.86	0.72	0.67	0.82	-0.76	-1.70*	-1.15	-0.20
	β_{11}	-0.0461	-0.044	0.0319	0.118***	0.219***	0.197***	0.246***	0.111***
	β_{12}	0.524***	0.441***	0.334***	0.201***	0.0927**	-0.0329	-0.0556	0.199***
	$H_0: \beta_{11}=\beta_{12}$	-5.13***	-4.07***	-5.55***	-1.58	1.52	2.11**	2.99**	-2.43**
	β_{21}	-0.0863***	-0.0805***	-0.0311*	-0.0180*	-0.00279	0.0318	0.0565**	-0.0224*
	β_{22}	0.0106	0.00784	-0.0123	-0.0314**	-0.0412***	-0.0313	-0.0719*	-0.0198*
	$H_0: \beta_{21}=\beta_{22}$	-1.97**	-2.01**	-0.74	0.75	1.70*	1.64*	2.16**	-0.13
	β_{31}	-0.0744***	-0.0569***	-0.0459***	-0.0348***	-0.0272***	-0.0124	-0.00775	-0.0387***
	β_{32}	-0.0601***	-0.0453***	-0.0222***	-0.0219***	-0.0267***	-0.0113	-0.00464	-0.0246***
	$H_0: \beta_{31}=\beta_{32}$	-0.74	-0.64	-3.36***	-2.04**	-0.05	-0.09	-0.14	-2.25**
	β_{41}	-0.00340***	-0.00286**	-0.000726	0.000142	0.000329	0.00043	0.000218	-0.000692
	β_{42}	0.00136	0.000665	-8.79E-06	-0.000526	-0.00091	0.000101	0.000357	-0.000195
	$H_0: \beta_{41}=\beta_{42}$	-2.26**	-1.82*	-0.82	0.88	1.32	0.20	-0.06	-0.61

IN	β_{11}	0.0218	0.0239	0.0793*	0.221***	0.328***	0.547***	0.536***	0.283***
	β_{12}	0.755***	0.660***	0.408***	0.267***	0.177***	0.0447	-0.0258	0.199***
	$H_0: \beta_{11} = \beta_{12}$	-4.97***	-5.02***	-3.55***	-0.71	2.26**	5.25***	5.06***	-1.64*
	β_{21}	-0.0554	-0.0765***	-0.0603***	-0.0238**	-0.0162	-0.0216	-0.031	-0.0373***
	β_{22}	0.0297	0.0303	-0.0012	-0.0303***	-0.0381**	-0.0548***	-0.0215	-0.0217*
	$H_0: \beta_{21} = \beta_{22}$	-1.29	-2.52**	-2.21**	0.41	0.84	0.85	-0.18	-0.79
	β_{31}	-0.113***	-0.0884***	-0.0612***	-0.0416***	-0.0377***	-0.0322***	-0.0229	-0.0573***
	β_{32}	-0.0409***	-0.0349**	-0.0228**	-0.0239***	-0.0286***	-0.0356***	-0.0332***	-0.0353***
	$H_0: \beta_{31} = \beta_{32}$	-3.37***	-4.00***	-5.76***	-2.62**	-1.34	0.38	0.56	-3.47***
	β_{41}	-0.002	-0.000642	0.000317	-0.000148	1.49E-05	-0.000931	-0.000509	-0.000823*
	β_{42}	-0.00247***	-0.00198**	-0.00131**	-0.00138	0.000398	0.00111**	0.00185***	-0.000478
	$H_0: \beta_{41} = \beta_{42}$	0.29	1.17	1.70	-0.01	-0.46	-1.90*	-1.80*	-0.42
IT	β_{11}	-0.0245	-0.055	0.0498	0.109***	0.154***	0.332***	0.265***	0.109***
	β_{12}	0.568***	0.489***	0.385***	0.179***	0.0687	-0.0157	-0.0716	0.210***
	$H_0: \beta_{11} = \beta_{12}$	-4.79***	-5.42***	-3.79***	-1.19	1.04	3.36***	2.31**	-2.01**
	β_{21}	-0.139**	-0.154***	-0.0804***	-0.0346***	0.00657	0.0660**	0.170**	-0.0307*
	β_{22}	0.161	0.133***	0.0179	-0.0221*	-0.0457**	-0.117**	-0.119**	-0.0156
	$H_0: \beta_{21} = \beta_{22}$	-2.01**	-4.61***	-3.23***	-0.64	1.65*	2.74***	2.77***	-0.56
	β_{31}	-0.102***	-0.0676***	-0.0684***	-0.0465***	-0.0307***	-0.0344***	-0.0256***	-0.0503***
	β_{32}	-0.0339	-0.0131	-0.0181	-0.0083	-0.0109	0.0109	0.027	-0.0116*
	$H_0: \beta_{31} = \beta_{32}$	-2.21**	-2.38**	-3.88***	-3.84***	-1.67*	-3.27***	-3.18***	-4.44***
	β_{41}	-0.00511**	-0.00254**	-0.000262	-0.000556	-0.00146**	-0.00182	-0.000612	-0.00151**
	β_{42}	-0.00177	-0.000085	-0.000768	-8.74E-06	0.00112*	0.000928	-0.0011	4.83e-05
	$H_0: \beta_{41} = \beta_{42}$	-1.10	-0.74	0.40	-0.63	-2.60***	-1.34	0.14	-1.38
MT	β_{11}	0.204***	0.197***	0.233***	0.372***	0.524***	0.665***	0.789***	0.426***
	β_{12}	0.776***	0.714***	0.575***	0.408***	0.262***	0.162***	0.0615	0.442***
	$H_0: \beta_{11} = \beta_{12}$	-5.62***	-8.19***	-7.00***	-0.61	5.23***	5.97***	8.11***	-0.50
	β_{21}	-0.0884***	-0.0727***	-0.0531***	-0.0270**	0.0104	0.0158	-0.0121	-0.0238**
	β_{22}	0.00801	0.0016	-0.0192	-0.0274**	-0.0592***	-0.0742***	-0.0643***	-0.0363***
	$H_0: \beta_{21} = \beta_{22}$	-1.91*	-1.97*	-1.53	0.02	3.24***	3.26***	1.02	0.72
	β_{31}	-0.108***	-0.0948***	-0.0686***	-0.0623***	-0.0533***	-0.0507***	-0.0556***	-0.0680***
	β_{32}	-0.0642***	-0.0591***	-0.0398***	-0.0422***	-0.0468***	-0.0407***	-0.0440***	-0.0458***
	$H_0: \beta_{31} = \beta_{32}$	-2.01**	-4.16***	-3.37***	-3.57***	-1.19	-1.15	-1.01	-3.93***
	β_{41}	-0.000654	-0.000156	9.36E-05	0.000111	-0.000536	-0.000328	0.000158	-0.000259
	β_{42}	-0.00153	-0.000923	-0.000685	-0.00036	0.000682	0.00114**	0.00142	-0.000177
	$H_0: \beta_{41} = \beta_{42}$	0.56	0.70	0.98	0.58	-1.39	-1.45	-1.01	-0.11
RE	β_{11}	0.0301	0.0369	0.0824***	0.195***	0.351***	0.548***	0.669***	0.281***
	β_{12}	0.842***	0.663***	0.416***	0.275***	0.143***	0.0312	-0.0156	0.331***

$H_0: \beta_{11} = \beta_{12}$	-5.60***	-5.09***	-4.50***	-1.63*	2.70**	3.20***	4.46***	-1.06
β_{21}	-0.0279	-0.0289	-0.0544***	-0.0516**	-0.0423	-0.0628**	-0.111***	-0.0520***
β_{22}	-0.0501	-0.00812	0.00198	-0.0136	-0.0341**	-0.0123	-0.0198	-0.0138
$H_0: \beta_{21} = \beta_{22}$	0.36	-0.69	-2.59**	-1.15	-0.25	-1.19	-2.03**	-1.51
β_{31}	-0.121***	-0.0610***	-0.0512***	-0.0376***	-0.0451***	-0.0407***	-0.0354***	-0.0548***
β_{32}	-0.0499***	-0.0402***	-0.0261***	-0.0267***	-0.0327***	-0.0333***	-0.0361***	-0.0355***
$H_0: \beta_{31} = \beta_{32}$	-2.43*	-0.96	-2.92**	-0.96	-1.47	-0.53	0.04	-2.36**
β_{41}	-0.00407**	-0.00111	-0.000845	-0.00108**	-0.00108*	-0.00231**	-0.00282***	-0.00171***
β_{42}	-0.000754	-0.00157	-0.00031	0.000122	0.00101**	0.0024	0.00121	0.000478
$H_0: \beta_{41} = \beta_{42}$	-1.49	0.27	-0.50	-1.71*	-2.14**	-2.13**	-2.41**	-2.07**
TL β_{11}	-0.0873	0.0522	0.152***	0.241***	0.261***	0.368***	0.368***	0.225***
β_{12}	0.560***	0.436***	0.331***	0.187***	0.116***	-0.0311	-0.0503	0.184***
$H_0: \beta_{11} = \beta_{12}$	-6.70***	-3.97***	-3.25***	1.17	3.11***	5.22***	3.89***	1.15
β_{21}	-0.0733***	-0.0783***	-0.0450***	-0.0443***	-0.00209	0.0335	0.0996***	-0.0287**
β_{22}	0.0752***	0.0852***	0.0113	-0.0335***	-0.0721***	-0.0992***	-0.0833***	-0.0178
$H_0: \beta_{21} = \beta_{22}$	-4.23***	-3.97***	-1.81*	-0.35	2.13**	2.87***	4.28***	-0.57
β_{31}	-0.0867***	-0.0691***	-0.0505***	-0.0339***	-0.0188***	-0.00952*	-0.00866	-0.0364***
β_{32}	-0.0343***	-0.0297***	-0.0261***	-0.0228***	-0.0264***	-0.013	-0.0237	-0.0259***
$H_0: \beta_{31} = \beta_{32}$	-2.31**	-2.72***	-2.28**	-2.06**	1.11	0.43	0.91	-1.72*
β_{41}	-0.000365	0.000478	0.000561	0.00022	0.000797	0.000973	0.00105	0.000375
β_{42}	-0.000381	-0.000121	7.90E-05	0.000215	0.000139	-0.000537	0.000225	0.000158
$H_0: \beta_{41} = \beta_{42}$	0.01	0.57	0.50	0.01	1.05	1.07	0.44	0.27
UT β_{11}	-0.0476	-0.0149	0.134***	0.266***	0.333***	0.381***	0.383***	0.241***
β_{12}	0.704***	0.568***	0.398***	0.279***	0.211***	0.101***	-0.0281	0.315***
$H_0: \beta_{11} = \beta_{12}$	-4.10***	-6.55***	-4.68***	-0.28	2.66***	4.72***	3.15***	-1.97**
β_{21}	-0.122***	-0.108***	-0.0650***	-0.0510***	0.00574	0.0297**	0.0561	-0.0419***
β_{22}	0.0721***	0.00903	-0.0141	-0.0502***	-0.0555***	-0.0744***	-0.0932***	-0.0395***
$H_0: \beta_{21} = \beta_{22}$	-4.02***	-2.54**	-2.18**	-0.06	2.09**	3.04***	2.56**	-0.12
β_{31}	-0.0945***	-0.0880***	-0.0575***	-0.0401***	-0.0354***	-0.0346***	-0.0240**	-0.0500***
β_{32}	-0.0730***	-0.0583***	-0.0355***	-0.0355***	-0.0286***	-0.0336***	-0.0288***	-0.0407***
$H_0: \beta_{31} = \beta_{32}$	-1.23	-2.43**	-2.53**	-0.65	-0.95	-0.10	0.27	-1.44
β_{41}	-0.00235	-6.13E-05	-8.01E-05	0.000147	0.000403	-0.000557	-0.000991	-0.000390
β_{42}	0.00135	-0.000147	-9.60E-05	-0.00024	-0.000114	0.000934	0.00149	7.01E-05
$H_0: \beta_{41} = \beta_{42}$	-1.45	0.06	0.02	0.43	0.57	-1.10	-1.21	-0.55

Note: The estimation results are reported for Equation (5) and (9). The 10%, 5% and 1% significance levels are denoted by *, ** and *** respectively.

Table 4.5. Quantile slope equality for positive and negative oil and EPU shocks

		\multicolumn{2}{c}{0.05 against the other quantiles}									
		0.50	0.95		0.50	0.95		0.50	0.95		0.50	0.95
EM	β_{11}	-3.22***	-4.48***	β_{12}	3.62***	6.92***	β_{21}	-1.17	-2.45**	β_{22}	1.89*	1.60
CD	β_{11}	-2.16**	-4.81***	β_{12}	4.00***	5.12***	β_{21}	-1.53	-2.63***	β_{22}	2.45***	2.43***
CS	β_{11}	-3.94***	-4.99***	β_{12}	2.72***	5.22***	β_{21}	-1.61*	-1.78*	β_{22}	2.64***	3.17***
EY	β_{11}	-6.60***	-6.66***	β_{12}	3.34**	6.08***	β_{21}	-2.04**	-2.96**	β_{22}	1.38	1.98**
FN	β_{11}	-1.96**	-4.17***	β_{12}	5.02***	9.13***	β_{21}	-0.90	-2.97**	β_{22}	1.42	2.34**
HC	β_{11}	-2.55**	-3.66***	β_{12}	3.99**	7.13***	β_{21}	-2.10**	-3.36***	β_{22}	1.53	1.62*
IN	β_{11}	-2.35**	-5.91***	β_{12}	6.19***	7.50***	β_{21}	-0.70	-0.47	β_{22}	1.54	1.05
IT	β_{11}	-1.54	-2.76***	β_{12}	3.53***	3.94***	β_{21}	-1.90*	-2.95***	β_{22}	1.84*	2.70***
MT	β_{11}	-2.18**	-6.51***	β_{12}	4.45***	6.49***	β_{21}	-1.55	-1.70*	β_{22}	1.68*	1.95**
RE	β_{11}	-2.34**	-5.05***	β_{12}	5.30***	6.69***	β_{21}	0.56	2.41***	β_{22}	-0.96	-0.75
TL	β_{11}	-4.81***	-5.22***	β_{12}	7.45***	8.46***	β_{21}	-0.88	-3.93***	β_{22}	3.75***	6.31***
UT	β_{11}	-3.26***	-3.67***	β_{12}	3.82***	5.13***	β_{21}	-2.25**	-3.83***	β_{22}	5.20***	3.93***

		\multicolumn{2}{c}{0.05 against the other quantiles}									
		0.50	0.95		0.50	0.95		0.50	0.95		0.50	0.95
EM	β_{31}	-4.26***	-5.57***	β_{32}	-0.92	-1.41	β_{41}	-0.22	1.06	β_{42}	-1.67*	-3.26***
CD	β_{31}	-5.40***	-5.08***	β_{32}	-0.49	-0.55	β_{41}	-1.27	-1.31	β_{42}	-1.96**	-3.45***
CS	β_{31}	-4.40***	-4.43***	β_{32}	-0.61	0.54	β_{41}	-2.64***	-1.92*	β_{42}	0.43	-1.19
EY	β_{31}	-2.64***	-2.96***	β_{32}	-0.54	-0.42	β_{41}	-1.17	-0.94	β_{42}	1.19	0.26
FN	β_{31}	-4.97***	-4.14***	β_{32}	-2.42**	-3.16***	β_{41}	-1.04	-0.11	β_{42}	-2.37**	-3.87***
HC	β_{31}	-2.51**	-2.92***	β_{32}	-1.82*	-2.55**	β_{41}	-2.98***	-1.91*	β_{42}	1.75*	0.70
IN	β_{31}	-7.86***	-5.65***	β_{32}	-0.90	-0.32	β_{41}	-1.15	-0.82	β_{42}	-3.91***	-6.16***
IT	β_{31}	-2.13**	-2.56***	β_{32}	-1.31	-2.84***	β_{41}	-2.07**	-1.42	β_{42}	-1.23	-0.27
MT	β_{31}	-3.16***	-3.06***	β_{32}	-2.40**	-1.98**	β_{41}	-0.80	-0.66	β_{42}	-1.16	-2.86***
RE	β_{31}	-3.76***	-3.67***	β_{32}	-1.40	-0.79	β_{41}	-1.71*	-0.62	β_{42}	-0.57	-1.39
TL	β_{31}	-3.03***	-3.80***	β_{32}	-0.75	-0.55	β_{41}	-0.48	-0.76	β_{42}	-0.70	-0.42
UT	β_{31}	-3.80***	-4.73***	β_{32}	-3.11***	-2.62**	β_{41}	-1.52	-0.75	β_{42}	1.12	-0.09

Note: The 10%, 5% and 1% significance levels are denoted by *, ** and *** respectively.

4.5. Conclusions

This examines the asymmetric impact of oil and EPU shocks on the emerging markets composite sectoral equity indexes. The novel shock decomposition approach of Ready (2018) is used to disentangle the oil price changes into the oil demand, supply and risk shocks. The finds that the demand shocks are positively related to stock returns, however, the supply, risk and EPU shocks are negatively associated with stock returns. The stock returns are mainly vulnerable to these shocks at the bearish market conditions. Further, the author also investigates the asymmetric exposure of stock returns to these shocks and finds that the lower demand shocks are associated with higher returns. Besides, the higher supply, risk and EPU shocks have more intense impact on stock returns than otherwise. Hence, the documents the evidence of asymmetric relationship of oil and EPU shocks with stock returns. Additionally, the slope of the coefficients also differs across all the quantiles, which essentially means that the sensitivity of the stock returns changes across the state of the market. The author believes the results are interesting and useful to international portfolio managers, policy makers and other stakeholders.

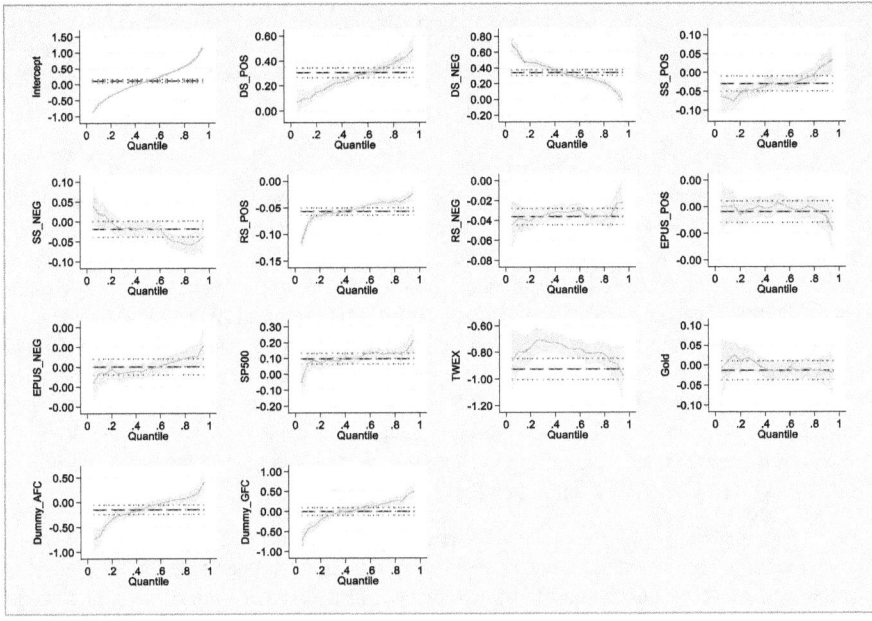

Figure 4.2. Coefficient plot of OLS and quantile regression
Note: The figure exhibits the estimates of OLS and coefficients of quantile regression for the aggregate emerging markets for Equation (8), the predictor variables indicated on the vertical axis. The broken black and the dotted horizontal lines represent the coefficient of OLS at its 95% confidence intervals respectively. The shaded areas around the quantile regression coefficient plotline represent the confidence interval at 95%.

CHAPTER 5

SUMMARY OF FINDINGS AND SCOPE FOR FUTURE RESEARCH

This chapter summarizes the findings of the three essays and discusses the scope for the future studies. The focusses upon the impact of the global risk factors upon the stock prices in the emerging markets. Thus, the author focuses upon some relevant exogenous sources of shocks based on recent literature and studies its impact upon the stock markets. The is bifurcated in three independent essays that emphasizes upon the impact of Economic Policy Uncertainty (EPU), Geopolitical Risks (GPR), Financial Stress (FS) and oil shocks upon the stock markets. The first essay deals with the causal relationship in mean and variance between the US based EPU, GPR and FS with the stock returns in 24 emerging markets. The second essay examines the relationship between the oil price shocks and 24 emerging markets. Finally, the third essay investigates the asymmetric impact of the oil and EPU shocks on the sectoral emerging market equity returns.

The first essay finds the evidence of heterogeneous impact of EPU, GPR and FS shocks upon the stock returns across the markets in terms of the magnitude of the causality. Additionally, it is also documented that the influence of EPU is mostly profound and significant as compared to other two shock indicators i.e. GPR and FS. Moreover, the causality-in-mean is more significant and stronger rather than the causality-in-variance i.e. the price risk is higher than the variance risk. Lastly, the predictability of EPU, GPR and FS is comparatively strong in lower tails. Though the adds some value to the existing literature, nevertheless, there remain possibilities to extend the present and add new dimensions to the literature. Such as, it is difficult to negate the fact that US based shocks are propagated to the other parts of the economy through certain channels of investments, trade linkages, political agreements etc. These channels could be the effective to determine the vulnerability or sensitivity of stock markets to the respective nature of shocks. Thus, as a future course of this question could be taken into consideration. Hence, a deeper understanding of the facts such as: if an economy is more influenced by US based EPU/GPR/FS, what are the possible channels? What are possible determinants? The author believes these questions are thought provoking and may be undertaken as future studies.

The second essay revisits the impact of oil shocks upon the emerging equity markets by using the novel shock decomposition algorithm proposed by Ready (2018). The finds that the relationship stock returns and demand shocks is positive, whereas the supply shocks are negatively related with exception to some of the oil-exporting countries. The risk-based shocks also have negative association with stocks. The fails to find the evidence of strong regime dependence and the direction of relationship across the high and low regimes is stable. The author also documents the intense oil-stock relationship in bearish market conditions. Besides, the also reports certain evidences of alterations of the oil-stock relationship onset the Global Financial Crisis (GFC) of 2008. Though the author believes that this is insulated of some of the limitations of the prior studies, nonetheless, there remains several other facets of the oil-stock relationship which may be considered for future investigation. There is every possibility that the vulnerability of the markets to oil price shocks may depend on the stage of market growth and business cycle, which may be examined explicitly. In addition, examination of sector-specific sensitivity of stocks may also be done in the context of emerging markets. Another important research avenue could be the investigations of asymmetric exposure of the stocks to the various sources of oil shocks. Furthermore, the consideration of other exogeneous factors in a multifactor asset pricing model framework such as country risks, policy uncertainty along with oil shocks could also be viewed as a potential sphere of future research.

Finally, the third essay examines the asymmetric impact of oil and economic policy uncertainty shocks on the emerging markets composite sectoral equity indexes. The author finds that the demand shocks are positively related to stock returns, however, the supply, risk and EPU shocks are negatively associated with stock returns. The stock returns are mainly vulnerable to these shocks at the bearish market conditions. Further, the author also investigates the asymmetric exposure of stock returns to these shocks and reports that the lower demand shocks are associated with higher returns. Besides, the higher supply, risk and EPU shocks have more intense impact on stock returns than otherwise. Hence, the documents the evidence of asymmetric relationship of oil and EPU shocks with stock returns. As a future course of , the researchers may focus on the fact that the magnitude of oil and EPU shocks vary across the sectors. The sectoral sensitivities are determined by the inherent abilities of the sectors to transfer or absorb the oil price changes also determine the sensitivity of its stocks towards oil shocks (Arouri and Nguyen, 2010). Thus, the researcher may focus upon the various channels and market structure to assess the degree of oil and EPU risk exposure on stock returns.

The researcher believes that these findings are relevant to the individual and portfolio investors, policy-makers and other stakeholders in the emerging markets for the purpose of international portfolio diversification and developing investment strategies at times of turbulent economic conditions.

www.ingramcontent.com/pod-product-compliance
Lightning Source LLC
LaVergne TN
LVHW020425080526
838202LV00055B/5045